21

PILLARS OF POWER

Clear Steps to Spiritual & Personal Fulfillment that are Real, Relevant, and Relational

by

Dr. Lamont E. Ricks

Library of Congress Cataloging-in-Publishing Data

Note. This book is based on the author's interpretation and experiences. It is not designed to replace the Bible or any tool books used as study aids. It is not intended to replace licensed counseling services, psychiatric, or pastoral counseling. The reader assumes complete responsibility for consequences of any actions taken from the information presented in this book.

All Scripture references are taken from the New American Standard Bible ©1960, 1962, 1963, 1968, 1971, 1972, 1973, 1975, 1977, 1995 by the Lockman Foundation.

ISBN-13: 978-0615835655
ISBN-10: 0615835651

Printed in the United States of America

Cover Design by Amber Parker
Back Cover Photo by Carrie Sethman

Booking Information
To book Dr. Ricks for your next speaking event, please send an email request to: info@drricksempowers.com or drricksempowers@gmail.com

Follow Dr. Ricks on Twitter for motivational quotes:
@DrRicks2

DEDICATION

To my Lord and Savior, Jesus The Christ
To my beautiful wife and children
Leroy, Sr. and Vanessa Ricks
Mr. & Mrs. Sample
Leroy, Jr. and Lance
My nieces and nephew
Jason Harris
Alvin "Ducey" Jones
Curtis L. Parker
Dr. Immanuel Watkins, Sr. (Hebrew)
Mr. Adam Harrell, Sr.
Addie Beatrice Harrell (Momma-Bea)
The Late Ernestine Woodhouse (Nanny)
The Late Doris Hargrove (Mother Dear)
The Late Luther Weaver
Rev. Wayman C. Ashburne
Dr. Rudolph Ford, III
Eddie & Mary Clayton
The Hinton Family
The Ricks Family
New Berean
To all of you who hunger for a personal and spiritually fulfilled life.

God Bless You

Lamont

CONTENTS

God's View of You

Position Yourself: Letting Go of Dead Weight

Protect Yourself: Rising Above Adversity

Encourage Yourself: Tapping Into Your Power Source

Brace Yourself: Get Ready to Prosper

CONCLUSION

ABOUT THE AUTHOR

NOTES

GOD IS ABLE

POWER UP!

Introduction

Hello, my friend. Welcome to **21 Pillars of Power**, a *Mo-votional™* book that can be used for years to come, by both old and young readers. Now you may be thinking, *"mo-votional™?"* What is that? Well, it is a term that I coined as I was writing this book. There are many genres that books fall into, such as *motivational books, self-help books,* and *devotional books. God* gave me this term as I was reading over the several chapters. By definition, a *mo-votional™* book is the offspring of a *motivational* and a *devotional* book. It is the *culmination* of both categories into one source. It is designed to *charge* you up. It is also designed to *slow* you down so you can *ponder* every nugget of wisdom. Therefore, *21 Pillars of Power's* objective is to not only motivate and inspire (motivational) its readers, but to catalyze *self-evaluation* and *self-reflection* (devotional). If you are looking for a quick, yet powerful *illustration* of practical life principles, many of which are based *on* Biblical principles, then you have found the perfect book. I am so excited about *21 Pillars of Power* that I promise it will make a *significant difference* in the way you approach *life's problems, opportunities,* and *seasons of change.*

The number 21 means a lot to me. I chose this number for the following reasons: One, it takes approximately 21 days to *develop* a habit and it takes about 21 days to *break* a habit. Two, in the Bible, the prophet Daniel *fasted* and *prayed* for 21 days before the Angel of the Lord brought him *an answer* to his prayers. Isn't that what *life's journey* is all about, finding *answers* to our problems? In case you didn't know, you are on a journey from the cradle to the grave. The relationships you will develop, the love you will experience, the trials of life you will encounter, and the victories you will secure are all found on the road of life. The key, however, is learning how to *positively adjust* to the *circumstances of daily living.* Daniel was in a lot of spiritual, emotional, and mental anguish during the time of his fast, however, his fast developed strength, a clear purpose, and a deeper fellowship with God. You see, in this life you will face mountains, peaks, and valleys. You will face crises, frustrations, and disappointments. But God has established simplistic principles that are sure to assist you in every situation. I call them, the *21 Pillars of Power.* Power Up!

ACKNOWLEDGMENTS

First, I would like to thank my Lord and Savior, Jesus Christ, for dying on the cross for my sins. Equally important, I want to thank Him for allowing me to share my thoughts and passion with the world. I would like to thank all of the "prayer warriors" at New Berean Baptist Church in Portsmouth, Virginia who constantly sought the face of God on my behalf; I love you. Thank you for keeping the fire alive! I would like to thank Gerry Gaines, Dr. Jack Gaines and Rob Hill, Sr. for imparting the nuggets of wisdom I needed during the pioneering stages of writing this book. Finally, my design/media team, Amber Parker, Adam Parker, Ricky Lawrence, Carrie Sethman, and Sheena Griffin, you all are so gifted. God Bless. POWER UP!

PART I

GOD'S VIEW
OF YOU

Pillar 1: God, the Creator of the Universe!

"Do you not know? Have you not heard? The Everlasting God, the LORD, the Creator of the ends of the earth does not become weary or tired. His understanding is inscrutable."--Isaiah 40:28 (NASB)

That's right! It all starts with *God*. He deserves all of the credit. He has given mankind the gifts of *earthly dominion, wisdom,* and *knowledge of the inter-workings of the created world.* He has given us the gift of love, parenthood, emotional understanding, as well as the understanding of concepts, ideas, and realities. Man is *nothing* without God. That is, man is only a shell of dust and clay crafted to know God in this journey of life. Many times in life we quickly forget God watches over us, sparing us from our own selves. What do I mean by that? Basically, there have been times when God has spared us from the *stupid, crazy*, and/or *dangerous* decisions we made in our lives.

My grandmother always said "God looks out for *children* and *fools"* and boy we can *all* say that there were times we have been very *foolish* in our past. But God has protected us and kept us from the full blown consequences of our foolish behavior. What do we call this protective element of life? Well, some call it "*luck*", still others call it "*fate*", but I want to call it what the Bible calls it,

"GRACE." Grace is *undeserved favor*. Let's look at the following example:

The Cheating Wife

William is a hard-working, middle aged man (age 50) who loves his wife, Diane dearly. They have been married for 19 years and have two teenage daughters. William is a successful engineer at a local firm and has been promoted to managing partner. Diane, age 45, is a school teacher at a local high school and really enjoys the time she spends with the students. Working at the school allows Diane to re-live her *glory days* as a young and beautiful teenage girl. On the surface, Will and Diane seemed to have the perfect marriage. William makes sure he sends Diane flowers at work on a monthly basis. He takes her to exquisite restaurants, travels to exotic places with her for vacation, and pads her bank account with extra *spending* money. With William's new promotion at his firm, his income is more than enough to take care of Diane and the girls, leaving him with a few dollars to spare. With the extra income, he decided to plan a 20th anniversary trip for two to Hawaii and also purchased a $15,000 anniversary ring that incorporated Diane's birth stones alongside the diamonds.

William was in a great place in his life *until* he discovered the unthinkable. Diane was involved in a steamy love affair with Tariq, an award-winning football coach at her school. Tariq was a 32 year old, handsome gym teacher who had recently retired from the NFL. Having made millions of dollars during his illustrious 10-year NFL career, Tariq took the teaching job for the health benefits, not the money. One day, William took the day off to get some rest. While cleaning the home office, he stumbled across a 3-page love letter, hidden under Diane's old lesson plans. The love letter, written in his wife's handwriting, described in explicit *detail* the multitude of sexual acts, rendezvous after school hours, hotel room visits, lingerie purchases, and future plans to hook up with Tariq during Spring Break. As he *painfully* read Diane's words line-by-line, she exclaimed how Tariq was such a powerful, passionate, and exciting lover. She ended her love letter by articulating how *difficult* it was for her to concentrate on teaching when Tariq was in the building. William was beyond devastated. Like a speeding freight-train colliding with a man on a bicycle, William was crushed. His mind began to swim with emotions.

William lifted his head towards Heaven and cried out to God, *"Oh God, oh God, my God! What was the use of me being faithful all these years to her? God why didn't You stop this from happening?!!!"* A nauseating jolt attacked his stomach. He began to feel dizzy and disoriented. He thought of confronting his wife at the school. He thought of physically harming Diane out of rage. He thought of tormenting Tariq with his bare hands. He even thought of having an affair himself, just to show Diane that he could have pleasure with another woman. He asked himself, *"How could I have been so stupid not to see that something wasn't right with Diane?"* William was confused, hurt, angry, and

4

hopeless at the same time. He began to think about all of the times Diane said she had a parent conference after school. He thought about the times she said she had to work the ticket lines at the Friday night football games. He even thought about the times she was *too* tired to be intimate with him at night. William called on God for strength and totally surrendered to God's leading and guidance. As he beat his chest with his fists, he struggled to ask God to remove his hate for his wife and replace the hate with forgiveness. After a week of fasting and praying that God would convict his wife and strengthen his heart, William finally confronted Diane about the affair. Diane, full of fear and regret, told William that she could not rest because of her infidelity and decided to break it off with Tariq. She told William that she made a huge mistake and sinned greatly before God. She also told him she understood if he wanted a divorce because she didn't deserve a second chance for the indiscretion. William decided to kick Diane out of the house before he said or did something he would regret. Diane said she understood and reluctantly moved out. William cried for many nights, soaking his pillow with tears and cursing Diane's name. At times, against his convictions, he would drink himself to sleep because of the unbearable emotional pain. This rollercoaster ride lasted about seven months. It was hard for him to go to church knowing his marriage was in shambles, but he pressed his way to the house of God.

Even though it took many months for William to forgive Diane, God would not let William's love for his wife fizzle out. After hundreds of unreturned phone calls from Diane, changing the locks on the all of the doors of the house, and cancelling all of her bank account access, God started to shift William's heart back into her direction. Cautiously, he decided to give her another chance. Diane, full of remorse and regret, humbly returned to her husband. In an effort to prove her love for William, she quit her teaching job and sought intense therapeutic counseling to help her transition back into a marital relationship with William. Although the trip to Hawaii was reasonably cancelled, Diane was shocked by the $15,000 anniversary ring William presented to her at dinner. William said to her,

> *"Diane, you put me through Hell and high-water this past year, and to be honest, it's going to take years before I can completely recover. However, day by day, God is giving me the power to overcome all of the thoughts in my head of you and Tariq, Oh God, Diane, why, why, why? I forgive you and I love you more than you can ever know. I will love you until the day I die and this ring is a token of my love for you. I will never forget the pain you've caused me, but I will no longer bring it up. I want to move forward, with God's help."*

Diane, looking down in shame and regret, tearfully replied,

> *"William, I thought I knew what love was, but you have shown me the true meaning of love, mercy, and grace. I have caused you, the girls, and God great pain. I'm not worthy of a second chance. I will do whatever it takes to gain your trust. I vow to show you every day how appreciative I am of you with action, not just words."*

Now, some people would say "what kind of man is that?! Don't believe anything she says! She is going to play you for a sucker again, William! Are you out of your mind? Once a cheater, always a cheater!" Not so. William understood an eternal principle that many of us overlook on a daily basis. This principle is called grace. *Grace is undeserved favor.* Grace is never easy or simple, but often complex and painful. Like William, God has been treated like dirt by mankind. We turn our backs on His truth. We defy His laws, and we act as if He doesn't have a say so in our lives. Yet, because He loves the world so much, He patiently waits with open arms to clean up our lives, redirect our life's journey, and protect us from evil seen and unseen.

Do you know that *grace* is a daily necessity for us to live in a *fallen* world? How many times have you thought about things that did not line up with your character? How many times have you had *dark* thoughts about your enemies or haters of your destiny? How many times have you had *lustful, greedy,* or *mis-aligned* thoughts that never escaped out of your mouth? Reflect upon that for a minute. It is very easy for us to judge Diane, but there is no difference between Diane and many of us in the sight of God. Sin is sin. Whether in thought or in action, none of us have any right to point our boney finger at anyone caught up in a dark moment, period. I want to offer one critical caveat, however, the consequences can have various levels of expressions. Because of the grace of God, many of our selfish thoughts fail at becoming actions. You can *see* my actions, but you cannot see my thoughts about a situation. And if you act out negative thoughts and hurt people close to you, God will still provide grace for you. Now, do you see why *grace* is so important? *Grace* is never "earned," it is always "given." And the person who gives grace is "always" in a *superior* position to the person asking for it. Our friend, William, had every right to divorce his wife. He had every right to feel angry and upset. He invested his entire life into his marriage to Diane--only for her to waste it all on a tryst with a young handsome stud. God, the creator of the Universe felt a pain much greater than William. Imagine your chief creation (mankind) spitting in your face, cursing your name, and worshipping false gods. This is the rejection that God feels from mankind on a daily basis.

The Bible declares that man doesn't live by bread alone, but by every word that come from God's mouth (Matthew 4:4). God gives us life, health and strength, ability, intelligence, skills, protection from evil, blessings, and many freedoms--*only* for us to reject Him, curse Him, and say that He doesn't really exist. Do you know that He could wipe us off the map with a thought? That's like an ant talking trash to a 6 foot 8 inch football player, daring him to step on his ant hill. If a human baby can kill an ant with his or her pinky finger effortlessly, what do you think a grown man can do? This is how the human race compares to All Mighty God. We live our lives as if we are in full control when we are merely ants in God's world. If you are still breathing God's oxygen and can walk, talk, see, drive, and think, it is because of His grace. Period.

Discussion Questions

1. What is *grace*? Who gives grace?

2. How often do we need grace?

3. How did William show Diane grace?

4. How did Diane *respond* to the grace William gave to her?

5. Can you identify with William in some way? How?

6. Can you identify with Diane in some way? How?

7. Can you identify with Tariq in some way? Why or Why not?

8. Is there anyone in your past that you need to give grace to?

9. Is there anyone in your life who you need to ask for grace?

10. Look over your life and write out your thoughts about the *grace* that God has given you.

11. List examples of the times you received good things that you *did not* deserve?

Pillar 2: Identity Crisis: *Who* are You?

"I will give thanks to You, for I am fearfully and wonderfully made; Wonderful are Your works, and my soul knows it very well." –Psalms 139:14 (NASB)

When was the last time you *really* looked into the mirror? What did you see? Rather than ask, *what* do you see, the question is, "*Who*" do you see? Do you *see* a person of value? A person who has high *standards* and *expectations*? Do you see a person who has *gifts, talents,* and *special skills* that can make the world a better place? Do you see a person with a *voice* to be heard? If your answer is yes to these questions, then you are very close to knowing your true identity. A lot of us will never reach our full potential that God has already *programmed* for our lives because we don't know our *identity*. In my opinion, an **identity** *is the personal, psychological, physical, and spiritual picture of a person. Identity is expressed in a person's personality, speech, conversation, and actions within the framework of society.* A person's identity is rooted within a value assessment of him or herself. In other words, a person's overall worth. The overarching questions regarding identity are as follows: *Who am I when no one is around? Who am I in society at large? Who am I to those I enjoy being around?* Knowing your identity is a dynamic feature of human nature. The great Martin Luther King, Jr., Rosa Parks, Jackie Robinson, and Tony Dungy are some examples of *superb* individuals who knew their *true* identity. King knew he was a man *created* to be equal. Mrs. Parks knew she was a woman who *deserved* respect and equal treatment. Jackie knew he was just as good playing Major League Baseball as Joe DiMaggio and Mickey Mantle. Mr. Dungy knew that not only could he become a Super bowl winning coach, but his talent also inspired others, such as Super bowl winning coach Mike Tomlin (Pittsburgh Steelers). My friend, what am I getting at here? *Production* always *follows* potential. That is, you must "nail down" *who* you are and who you want to become before you can realize your dream.

The Chicken and the Eagle

There is a famous story by Dr. Eldon Taylor (2007) of an Eagle who fell from its nest as a fledgling. However, I would like add an imaginative twist to add emphasis, so aspects of the story will be different from the original. He landed on the ground, where two adult chickens discovered him. The chickens talked among themselves,

> *"Look at this baby chicken. He looks a little weird though. He is very dark with a white head. Let's take him back to the farmer's coop and nurse him back to health, for his wings are broken."*

So months went by and the baby Eagle began to grow at an alarming speed. Soon, the elder chickens realized that this weird young bird was no chicken at all, but an Eagle. The chickens congregated together and said, *"If he realizes that he is an Eagle, he may kill us! So what we will do is continue to make him feel as if he is just like us. As long as he believes that he is a chicken, he will not cause us any harm."* Hence, the chickens treated the young Eagle like a chicken, talked to him like a chicken, and influenced him to look at life from a chicken's point of view. They had indoctrinated the Eagle to expect food to come from the farmer, not to go out and search for it with all its heart and mind. *"That is what chickens do,"* replied a chicken towards the Eagle. *"We don't have to think about where our next meal is coming from. We just wake up at sunrise, walk around in the barn yard, and eat the corn when the farmer comes whistling."* The Eagle Replied, *"What if something happens to the old farmer, how will we eat?"* The chickens replied, *"The old farmer just seems to figure it all out."* The chickens went on to say, *"One day when you get older, the old farmer will give you two servings of corn kernels instead of only one serving."* Every day the old farmer would grab a bag of corn kernels and toss the kernels in the dirt for the chickens to eat. Like clockwork, the chickens, along with the Eagle, would rush from the coop and peck the corn, as if it were a steak dinner from an exquisite restaurant. Day after day, week after week, month after month, the chickens and the Eagle would do the same routine. However, on one fateful day, while eating their corn, they noticed two gigantic shadows hovering in a circle high above the farm. The chickens were so terrified that they all ran into the farmer's coop, but the Eagle, not knowing what was transpiring, simply looked up to the sky. To his surprise, he saw two huge black birds swooping down towards him. These strange birds landed right next to him and stated, *"Young boy, why are you down here with these measly chickens? Are you out of your mind?"* The young Eagle replied, *"No, I'm a chicken and this is who I am."* The adult Eagles said, *"Who told you this?"* The young Eagle said, *"My parents. They live in that coop over there."* The adult Eagles fell to the ground laughing, *"Boy, they are not your parents, they are chickens! Have you noticed that you do not look like them? Have you looked at your wings? Go ahead and spread your wings, son. See how wide they spread? They are for flying to un-earthly heights. Look at your feet, boy! Notice how sharp and long your talons are. They are created to tear apart flesh and rip bone. Do those chickens have talons?"* The young Eagle replied, *"No Sir, actually, they do not."* *"Feel your beak, son, do you see how it hooks into a razor sharp point? Your beak can rip through the toughest hide of any animal who opposes you. We are the kings of the air. God has given us dominion over all birds. There is no bird on Earth that can rival the Eagle and that is who you are, boy! In fact, Eagles eat other birds, such as chickens, for breakfast. This is why we came here; to eat. We didn't expect to see one of our own amongst our food. It's a good thing we stopped by today. You probably haven't flown in months have you?"* *"Fly?"* the young

Eagle replied. *"Yes, fly,"* said the older Eagles. *"Tell your chicken friends good-bye. Your home is 3,000 feet in the air. You have been limiting yourself all these years because you saw yourself as a chicken, son."* The young Eagle replied, *"I can't believe I've wasted so much of my time limiting myself in that chicken coop! Why didn't they tell me I was an Eagle?"* The older Eagles replied, *"Well, son, they knew that once you walked in your true identity, you would have left them behind in that dusty old coop. Besides, Eagles are very intimidating to a chicken. It may have made them feel better about themselves to have an Eagle seeking their advice."* The young Eagle replied, *"I am ready to go with you."*

The Eagle Mentality vs. The Chicken Mentality

Now, I can honestly say that this story is *relevant* to all of us, in some way or another. Many of us have *settled* for low achievement, reckless relationships, walking outside of our life's calling, dead-end jobs, and dead-beat friends--all because we've adopted a *chicken mentality*. A **chicken mentality** *is a state of mind in which one depends solely upon others he/she deems superior. It is a mindset in which one has the desire to achieve greater life goals, but lack a genuine belief and courage to overcome obstacles of limitation, criticism, and adversity. It is an orientation to only viewing one's self as "existing" within a prescribed social, economic, or physical role, as opposed to having the ability to "effect change" to his/her environment.* Individuals with a *Chicken mentality* are *convinced* that they cannot change their destination in life. They speak about change, but *refuse* to employ the steps necessary to make a change. However, a person with an *Eagle Mentality* is driven from within to change his or her environment towards a desired outcome. These individuals will not stop chasing their dreams because others *criticize, laugh,* or *mock* their ambitions. Those with an Eagle mentality are not at all embarrassed to ask the tough questions in order to secure the answers they need to reach their goals. They are willing to lose sleep, go into debt, or work several jobs to force their dreams to respond favorably. If you ever meet a person with an Eagle mentality, they have a laser-like focus that cannot be deterred by the mightiest of distractions. Don't expect to have a *high flying* Eagle life if you constantly surround yourself with *chickens*. All they do is a whole lot of *talking* about success, but fail to rise to the occasion. Now, let me caution you, it is very *comfortable* to have a *chicken mentality*. It takes a lot of grinding work to become an Eagle, but know this; God can give you strength to develop into a large Eagle. Get in the game and win what God has *already* ordained for you-*a fulfilled life*. This is the very reason we should constantly evaluate the people we *choose* to hang around, listen to, and follow. If a person cannot *add* to/*multiply* greatness in your life, or expose you to a *sophisticated* way of thinking and acting, then you may be in fellowship with a *chicken mentality* disciple. Do not believe the lie that you are merely a chicken with *limitations*. Limitations are only *illusions* designed to subjugate (oppress) the human mind-*the most powerful tool on Earth*. Remember, you only get *one* shot at living on this Earth, why not invest in your identity by chasing greatness in the lane God has placed before you? Say good-bye to the chickens and hello to the Eagles!

Identity Development

It is my belief that self-image derives from three sources **(1)** ***Home environment*, (2) *Society at large*, and (3) *Self*.** Many of the persons we meet with low self-image were *not born* with this condition, but were immersed in an *environment* of unhealthy comparison or competitiveness with others. Whether it was an unprofessional school teacher, a neglectful parent, or an insecure spouse, our self-image is *shaped* by the *words* and *actions* of the people we deem *significant*. However, there is good news; just because someone or some event in your life *crushed* your self-image, it can be *re-conditioned,* and in some cases, *resurrected*. Although this is *not* an overnight process, with time, effort, coaching, and personal responsibility, your self-image *can* be repaired to its God-ordained state. First, you must *humble* yourself under the mighty hand of God and realize that He is real and He created you. This is one of the hardest things to do, but it is necessary to experience true freedom. Second, you must figure out what you are good at and what you would like to contribute to the world. Do you want to help the sick? Do you want to motivate people in a positive way? Do you want to cure sicknesses? Whatever is the idea, write it down on a piece of paper. Third, place this list on your bathroom mirror so you can review it every day and every night before you go to bed. Fourth, find an accountable, Eagle-istic person to share your goals and aspirations with and ask that they hold you accountable to your goals. Fifth, write down the names of people that subtract from your life, that is, those who you have deemed chicken disciples. Once you have identified these individuals, think of ways to minimize your contact with them. Remember, you *are* who you choose to hang around and whoever you hang around will transfer their negative traits to you. God *never* intended for a person to *feel inferior* to another human being. In America, we have this monumental statement in our Constitution, *"All men are created equal."* Now how one interprets that statement is subjective, but I choose to understand it "literally." All men (man, woman, boy, and girl; black, white, green, red, and brown) are indeed created equal. That is, God has given every man the skill, talents and special gifts to maximize the society s/he dwells. My question to you is, *"How are you making a significant impact in the world you are currently occupying?"* In order to make an impact, you have to have a sense of self-value and worth. When you tap into the precious pool of "I can-ness" you will discover strengths, talents, skill, and most importantly, power to influence and motivate others.

Table 1 . *Sources of Negative and Positive seeds that impact self image*

Source	_Negative Seeds_	_Positive Seeds_
Parent (home environment)	"You will *never* amount to anything."	"You can do whatever you put your mind to."
	"You are just like your no good father."	"Don't blame your father for your poor choices, it's up to you to achieve."
	"You are dumb as Oatmeal."	"Practice makes perfect, don't give up."
	"You're thinking above yourself, now."	"I am so proud of your accomplishments; hard work pays off."
	"You are getting fat as a pig."	"Your health is critical to enjoying life, try to cut back."
	"You're not the sharpest tool in the box."	"All of us struggle with something, but all of us are *great* at something."
	"Let somebody else do it, and then you follow."	"Go after your dreams. You are the *only* one who can make your dream a reality...Launch out."

	"Just try to pass the class."	"Don't settle; you'll be settling for less the rest of your life."
Society at Large	"*Thin* is in."	"Beauty comes in all shapes, colors, and sizes, maximize your situation."
	"Everybody's doing it."	"Don't follow the crowd, *think* for yourself."
	"Don't be a prude."	"God is your most important audience, not man."
	"Get with the program."	"Get with God's program. It has eternal benefits."
	"*Long* Hair is beautiful."	"True beauty rests in our differences."
	"*Nothing* less than perfection."	"Although we should strive for excellence, none of us will *ever* be perfect in this fallen world. Do your *best* at all times."
	"It's a dog-eat-dog world."	"Trust in God's power to promote."
	"Sometimes you have to *sell* your soul to get what you want."	"Those who sell their souls become property of evil ambitions."

	"Everybody has a price."	"Your value is priceless."
	"You are Ghetto."	"You can't control where you are from, but you have a lot of control on where you are *going*, with God's help."
Self	"I'm not pretty enough."	"I am beautiful because God made me..."
	"I'm not strong enough."	"I can do all things through Christ..."
	"I'm not smart enough."	"I can do all things through Christ..."
	"I'm not able."	"I am more than able with God's help."
	"My parents didn't achieve."	"You may have your parent's blood, but you have your *own* brain."
	"I'm not eloquent in speech."	"Moses wasn't either."

"I made *too* many mistakes in my past."	"I will acknowledge God in my decisions for direction this time and take a step of faith." (Prov. 3:5-7)
"I can't, I won't, and I haven't."	"If I don't try, I'm *guaranteed* to fail."

As you can see, whatever is planted in our psyche (mind) will produce a certain type of fruit or harvest. If you plant an apple seed then you can expect an apple tree. What farmer plants watermelon seeds and expects to grow corn? It's not going to happen. The seed *always* matches the tree. The seed represents the *belief* and the tree represents the *outcome* of the belief one has developed about life. If a person spends all of his or her childhood having "negative" seeds *planted*, then those seeds will grow into a tree of negativity in their lives. Instead, one should change those negative seeds into positive seeds, as noted in the Table 1. Realize that *God* is able and more than willing to assist you in your quest of walking in your true "identity." God has never created you to be negative or hopeless. This is totally against His nature.

Discussion Questions

1. When you look into the mirror, *who* do you see?

2. When you look into the mirror, who *should* you see?

3. How did God create us? (Ps. 139:14)

4. What are the three sources of low self-image described in this chapter?

5. Can a low self-image be repaired? Yes or No? How?

6. Is there anyone who has caused you have low self-esteem?

Pillar 3: God Loves You! Period.

"Love is the only thing that costs a lot and pays a lot at the same time."—Dr. Lamont Ricks

Water is expressed in three separate forms, each having a distinct function. For example water is the liquid form of H_2O. Steam is the gas form of H_2O. Finally, ice is the solid form of H_2O. Although distinctly different, each form listed above (liquid, gas, and solid) is 100% H_2O. In the same vein, we serve one God, expressed in three *distinct* persons. They are *God the Father*, *God the Son*, and *God the Holy Spirit*. Each Person is 100% God. We call this union the *God Head*. All three agree as one and move as one. God the Father is Spirit and He is 100% God. Jesus Christ is the God-Man and is 100 % God, and the Holy Spirit is 100 % God. God the Father sent His Son, Jesus, to Earth to die for the sins of the world; past, present, and future sins. When Christ was crucified on the cross, He satisfied the wrath of God. Christ rose from the dead and was seen of 500 followers. Christ ascended to Heaven to sit at God the Fathers' right hand. Christ sent the Holy Spirit as a *promise* to all who believe on His name. The Holy Spirit lives inside of every true believer in Jesus. This is what I mean by the unity of the God Head. *Christianity* is exclusively different from any other religion because it is, in essence, a relationship with the Living God. **I Peter 2:14** declares the following:

> and He Himself bore our sins in His body on the cross, so that we might die to sin and live to righteousness; for by His wounds you were healed. (NASB)

In **Matthew 26:42** the Word declares:

> He went away a second time and prayed, "My Father, if it is not possible for this cup to be taken away unless I drink it, may your will be done." (NASB)

In **Matthew 20: 21-23** it powerfully states:

> "What is it you want?" he asked. She said, "Grant that one of these two sons of mine may sit at your right and the other at your left in your kingdom." "You don't know what you are asking," Jesus said to them. "Can you drink the cup I am going to drink?" "We can," they answered. Jesus said to them, "You will indeed drink from my cup, but to sit at my right or left is not for me to grant. places belong to those for whom they have been prepared by my Father." (NASB)

Take a moment to ponder upon the aforementioned verses. God has gone to the eternal limits of redeeming mankind back unto Himself. He left a perfect place (heaven) to come to this depraved world, only to be beaten, mocked, ridiculed, spit upon, cursed, blasphemed, and scourged by His creation. Basically, it is equivalent to a man running into a burning building to save a criminal that recently held him at gunpoint in cold blood. That is how much God loves us! His

love is like bleach. It can clean the toughest soil stain that sin
causes in our lives.

> *"For God so loved the world, that He gave His only
> begotten Son, that whoever believes in Him shall not
> perish, but have eternal life."*--John 3:16 (NASB)

There are several types of love; *Phileo, Eros, and Agape*
to name a few. *Phileo* means "brotherly love," or the endearing
love one would have for a brother or friend. *Eros* means
romantic love. This is showcased by those emotionally
charged "butterfly" feelings one would have for a "lover." This
type of love is deeper and richer than "Phileo" love. Lastly,
there is *Agape* love. God Himself demonstrates this type of
love. Agape love is demonstrated when a mother loves her
wayward child. No matter how deep the child plummets into a
disrespectful, vile, and wicked lifestyle, that mother holds a
place for him or her in her heart for redemption. However,
with God, *all* He (God) knows is "agape" love. This is what
makes a *personal* relationship with God so special and
significant. He *will* forgive us for *anything* we have done. He
even gives us *grace* when what we really deserve is severe
punishment. Nevertheless, I want to introduce a caveat (a
caution). Grace and forgiveness *do not* (1) give us permission
(license) to live in total contradiction to the Word of God (sin
freely), or (2) remove the "consequences" of a disobedient
lifestyle. When we approach Jesus (God) as our Lord and

Shepherd, we must be sure not to confuse Him with (a) a genie and (b) a passive liberalistic Deity. He is *Holy God*! This means that He *cannot* and will not *condone* sin, but he does forgive *all* sin. God *hates* sin, but loves the sinner, no matter how *vile, dirty, common*, or *rancid* the sin. For example, let's go back to the *married couple* in *chapter 1*. Although William *forgave* his cheating wife, he is cautious not to let her take advantage of him again. He did *not* condone what Diane had done. Think about it for a minute. She had several intense sexual encounters with *another* man, deceived her husband, and *leased* her marriage vows to a younger lover (Tariq). Her illicit behavior deeply scarred William. Nevertheless, with prayer, fasting, intense marital counseling, consistently reading God's Word (Bible), and surrendering himself completely to God's guidance, he was able to filter through all the *emotional* and *psychological* sewage, in order to reach the core of Diane's heart.

Let me illustrate this principle further. Suppose you attended a baseball game on Friday night and you really had to use the porter potty. Somehow, you *dropped* your *only* set of car keys and your wallet into the toilet and there was no mechanism available for you to retrieve them other than your hands. What would you do? Would you just leave your keys and wallet in the toilet, or would you go against all logic and sanitation and plunge your hands into the nasty toilet to

retrieve these precious items? Well, it depends on if you want
to make it back home that night. *No one* wants to place their
hands in a smelly, disease infested toilet, but sometimes you
have to do what you have to do and face tough issues heads
up. God, being purely Holy and full of love, grace, mercy, and
light did not want to face sin and death, but He did it out of
agape love! The only way God could redeem us from the slave
market of sin was to give His life on the cross and take our
place. He was willing to face eternal sin and the ills of fallen
man in order to give us another chance to live with Him in
Heaven! Wow, if that doesn't make you shed a tear, I don't
know what will. He died on a rugged cross for all mankind
once and for all. He loves us so much.

1 Peter 1:18 says,

> *"For Christ also died for sins once for all, the just for the
> unjust, so that He might bring us to God, having been
> put to death in the flesh, but made alive in the spirit;"*
> (NASB)

God loved the World so much that He wrapped Himself into
human flesh to bare the sins of all mankind, both past and
present and for all time! This act is called the *Incarnation*,
meaning God robed Himself in the *likeness* of human flesh, yet
without sin. Jesus, Who is God in the *Flesh,* had to shed His
blood for our sins. He was the only one who could fulfill the
wrath of God and payment of sin. When Adam sinned against

God in **Genesis chapter 3** in the Bible, our relationship with
God was severed (broken). Jesus Christ is the bridge between
fallen man and a Holy God. However, it's up to you to choose
to serve Jesus. He proved His *agape* love by drinking the
infamous "bitter cup." **Matthew 26:38-40** states:

> *Then He *said to them, "My soul is deeply grieved,*
> *to the point of death; remain here and keep watch*
> *with Me." And He went a little beyond them, and fell*
> *on His face and prayed, saying, "My Father, if it is*
> *possible, let this cup pass from Me; yet not as I will,*
> *but as You will." And He *came to the disciples and*
> **found them sleeping, and *said to Peter, "So, you*
> *men could not keep watch with Me for one hour?*
> (NASB)

Now someone may say, what is this "bitter cup?" Well, Christ
did not "literally" drink a bitter cup. Figuratively, the "bitter
cup" describes the agony He faced while anticipating the
crucifixion upon Calvary's cross. Let me drive this truth home
by using a little imagery. Following is a list of sins and
wickedness that a Holy, blameless, and Righteous God, who
was *without* sin, had to endure as a means of "buying" us back
from the slave market of Sin.

The Bitter Cup (Matthew 26:38-40)

Table 2: *The Bitter Cup of Mankind's depravity and fallen nature*

Murder	Gluttony	Pride	Rape
Greed	Jealousy & Hatred	Gossip	Disobedience to Parents
Witchcraft & Sorcery	Idol worship	Lying & Deception	Cheating
Racism	Bestiality	Genocide	Elitism
Divorce	Abuse	Drug Abuse	Depression
Sexual Perversion	Lust	Adultery	Prostitution
Abandonment	Molestation & Incest	Slander	Social Injustice

**Note: This is just an example of *some* of mankind's struggles based on the Bible. This is not an exhaustive list.

Again, **Table 2** only shows a *small* number of specific "sins" of outlined in the Holy Bible. The list of items that Jesus had to "drink" far exceeds what this book is capable of printing. *This is what I call love!* However, man must make an intelligent decision to accept the "*finished*" work of Christ Jesus in order to be redeemed or "*bought back*" by God; and the benefit, eternity in Heaven enveloped in eternal peace, joy, and tranquility with our Savior!

Discussion Questions

1. What are the 3 types of love described in this chapter?

2. At what lengths did God go to "buy mankind" back unto Himself?

3. How can you show "agape" love towards others?

4. How can you demonstrate love for others on a daily basis?

5. Is true "agape" love based on conditions?

PART II

POSITION YOURSELF: LETTING GO OF DEAD WEIGHT

Pillar 4: Association can Lead to Your Devastation

"The LORD said to Moses, "How long will this people spurn Me? And how long will they not believe in Me, despite all the signs which I have performed in their midst? "I will smite them with pestilence and dispossess them, and I will make you into a nation greater and mightier than they."--Numbers 14:11-12 (NASB)

There is an old adage that states "Birds of a feather flock together." Usually this statement is used to confirm that an individual showcases the same character flaws or poor behavior of the ones he or she associates with. However, I would like to take this age-old truth to a new level of intellectual ground. It's okay to be of the same "feather", as long as you are running with *Eagles*, not *Vultures (Buzzards)*. Let me further explain what I am saying here. A vital part of our human nature and existence is *relationships*. God created us to have life-changing, fulfilling, dynamic, and prosperous relationships with our fellow man. In **Genesis 2**, God *even* said of Adam, "*It is not good for man to be alone, I will make a helpmeet for him.*" (NASB).

This was the origin of relationships between two created human beings. Now, there are various levels of relationships: (1) partnerships, (2) associations with constituents, and (3) intimate relationships. Intimacy is composed of many levels. These levels can include the intimacy between a child and parent, the intimacy between dear friends, and the intimacy of a romantic (Eros) relationship between a man and a woman. As you can see, relationships consist of a broad range of possibilities that influence each and every one of us during different stages of our lives. I have seen many of my childhood friends crash on the "road of life"; not because they, themselves, were reckless, but due to their *linkages* with the *wrong people*. I have a question for you. Are you hanging out with someone you *know* in your heart is not good for you? If so, you may need to re-evaluate your connection with this person or group of people. Don't fall for the deception!

We are quick to tell *young* people, particularly school-aged children to *choose* their friends carefully, but what about us as *adults*? Can you look back over your adult or young adult life and pinpoint that "unwise" association that caused you unnecessary pain and regret, mental agony, depression, *loss* of money, *loss* of family, or *loss* of freedom? I share with a lot of young people all of the time that "peer pressure" is even *greater* for an adult than it is for a teenager. Think about this for a second. When you were a teenager, you *still* lived in somewhat of a monitored setting. A *parent* or guardian was taking care of you and you may have had a curfew and many neighborly "eyes" watching your every move. However, as a *grown* man or woman (meaning, you *pay your own bills, pay your rent/mortgage,* and are *self-sufficient*), you call the shots. Whether you decide to read the *Word of God,* attend weekly church services, or go on a *hedonistic* adventure with a group of friends, it is totally up to you. Technically, adults can *override* their own inhibitions, without having to answer to a human agent (i.e. their parents). They *do not* have a curfew, nor are they forced to walk under the umbrella of the "moral boundaries" that were shaped by their parents. However, therein, lies the "deception of being a *grown* adult." As created beings, we are *all* accountable to *God,* the Creator. This is a powerful truth that can easily get lost in our decision making. As an adult, we *mistakenly* assume that we pulled ourselves up by our own *bootstraps,* when, in fact, it was God Almighty Who protected us from the *full-blown* consequences of our associations with bad influences. For some of us, we should have been *killed* at the nightclub by *that* stray bullet. For some of us, we should have contracted *that* deadly sexual transmitted disease (STD) when we were sleeping around. For some of us, we should be serving a long *prison* sentence for the crimes we have committed. *But God,* whose love can reach the deepest level of man's *depravity,* was the shield that *protected* us, even when we *associated* with fools, *wicked individuals,* and *whoremongers*. This is another example of God's *grace.* So next time you are invited to participate in a relationship with someone who *does not* respect, love, or fear

God, be careful! More importantly, God's grace *can be frustrated* and when that happens, no force on Earth can stop the consequences.

Discussion Questions

1. How can your associations become doorways to trouble?

2. Are we created to have relationships? Why?

3. Will God's grace *always* bail us out of our poor choices or decisions? Why or Why not?

4. What are some key characteristics that you should consider before you associate or partner with someone?

Pillar 5: Association Can Lead to Your Elevation

"Without consultation, plans are frustrated, but with many counselors they succeed."--Proverbs 15:22(NASB)

I cannot talk about the *bad* without also mentioning the *good* that life's relationships offer. Take a moment and just think about the *successful* people that you know in life, both near and afar. What do you think a *common denominator* is among this group of esteemed individuals? Well, I'll tell you: *connections* with other *successful* people. In my personal opinion, a **highly successful person** is one who will possess the following traits:

- *An unquenchable drive, confidence, clear direction, clarion vision,*
- *A knowledge of his or her identity,*
- *A consistent and developing work ethic,*
- *A clear understanding of high expectations,*
- *A willingness to sacrifice the good for the great,*
- *A willingness to defer instant gratification to accomplish a larger purpose,*
- *An understanding and fear of God and comfort in the skin he or she is in.*

This is a *good general definition.* You can find successful people *all over the world,* but can their success be marked as the *highest form* and is their success acceptable in the *eyesight* of God? Well, let's find out.

The Big Time

Elise has an undying love for music. Ever since she was a little girl, you would find her playing with instruments, singing in church, and mimicking her favorite music artists' voices. As Elise grew older, she had a strong desire to make it to the big time. She entered every local talent show, sent out her demo tapes, and met with local managers to showcase her powerful voice. But rejection, after rejection began to frustrate her to no end. Finally, she received a phone call from a talent agent who heard her demo tape. He told her how beautiful she sounded and that her voice was the missing link in his new female group's line up. He asked if she would fly up to New York to meet the record label, the group, and the famous producers who would be working on the debut album. Elise, full of excitement, fear, and tears, dropped the telephone to the ground. She tried to contain her emotions and began to quietly speak to herself,

> *"Girl, this is it! All of the rejection, all of the haters, all of my critics. Look at me now! Okay, girl, you can do this. This is your time. Just calm your nerves and pick up the phone. Don't sound too eager. Just book the flight to New York, baby."* Elise picks up the phone. *"Hello?"* *"Yes",* the agent replied. *"I will book the flight to New York. I am very thankful for the opportunity to meet you, the group, and the record label."*

Elise has finally broke into the music industry. She worked so hard to get recognized by the right people and now it has paid off. She took pride in the positive messages of her music. She even wrote her own lyrics. However, to her surprise, once she got her big break, part of her contract involved *promoting* her body as a selling point.

Now folks, there is *nothing* wrong with looking good and feeling good about your body. However, there is a *major* problem with projecting a *promiscuous, over-sexed* image to sell records to *young boys and girls*. After reading the terms of the contract, she began to struggle within.

> *"I've worked so hard to climb this steep mountain. Demo after demo, rejection after rejection, I am finally here. I've come too far to turn around and go back. I know it's wrong, but look at all of the doors this will open up for me to financially assist my family. The Lord knows my heart. I got to start at the bottom, right? I'll just do this for a few years launch my solo career and then I can call my own shots."*

Regretfully, she *agreed* to the contractual terms. She went on to sell *hundreds of thousands* of records and was invited to many exclusive, star-studded parties throughout her career. She was in a good financial place in her life and could buy whatever she wanted. So, my question to you, my friend is this: *Is Elise successful?* There are certain *elements* that qualify her as a success. She had *drive, confidence, ambition,* and *tremendous talent*. However, success should go beyond these necessary traits. When you are able to use your gifts, talents, and skills that are *acceptable* to God, you have reached the *highest level* of success that man can reach. Yes, Elise was successful, but the trade-off of leading young boys and girls down a path of promiscuity and lust far outweighs her personal success. The ***highest*** form of success is when (1) you win, (2) those you serve win, and (3) God wins. When all three of these elements are in order, you can truly say with confidence that you've reached the highest level of success.

Now that I've identified success, don't just hastily run out and try to attach yourself to successful people in order to secure *personal gain*. They will quickly detect your *selfish ambition* and *dismiss* you quicker than you can spit out sour milk. No, *kindred* spirits naturally connect and work together to achieve a *common* goal. You have to bring a skill set, talent or gift to the table before you can connect with a successful individual. For illustration, let's use the tandem of *Joe Montana* (#16) and *Jerry Rice* (#80) of the Super bowl winning San Francisco 49ers. Joe Montana is arguably in the top 10 of *all* NFL quarterbacks and Jerry Rice is arguably the *greatest wide receiver* ever. Although these fine athletes played over 10 seasons together, each had separate forms of *off-season* training, which was tailor-made for each person's position, personality, and assignment. If you want to connect, or build a strong network of associates who are "*movers and shakers*", then "you" have to develop a *personal plan* to make it happen. You have to become a *mover and shaker* too. That is, you have to "*create*", "*activate*", and "*execute*" your plan.

You must be willing to *push yourself* to study the inter-workings of your dream. You have to be willing to pray to God *without* stopping. You have to develop *patience* until your opportunity presents itself. You have to be *willing* to *defer* feeling embarrassed to get the questions you need answered. Maximize your potential by continuing to develop your goals and dreams and watch how God elevates you.

Pillar 6: Parasites vs. Parachutes

"I don't need drainers in my life, but people that's going to drive me!"--Pastor Terrance Johnson, Higher Dimension Church, Houston, Texas

When you run into a "misled, non-goal directed, lazy person", how do you respond? When you run into a "self-assured, positive, and encouraging individual", how do you respond? There are many types of people in this world, but two individuals you must be able to identify are the *parasites* and the *parachutes*. First, let's define the two in the simplest way. According to Webster's dictionary (2012), a **parasite** is: *a person who receives support, advantage, or the like, from another or others without giving any useful or proper return, as one who lives on the hospitality of others.*[1] You know the kind; they constantly want to hang around, but the stench of their poor choices, pessimistic attitudes, and inferior mind-set causes you frustration. Do you know anyone who would qualify as a *parasite*? I'm sure you do. Some of your family members may be *parasites*. You know who they are when you see them at a cookout or family reunion. Their famous words are,

> *"Cousin, let me hold something (money)". "You know the "MAN" is keeping me down and I'm hard on my luck and need some financial assistance".* Or, how about the person that says, *"Oh you think you are better than me?*

You're a big-time college graduate or business owner now? I remember when you couldn't find a job or get a mate.", "I remember when you had nothing!" "If it were not for me believing in you, you may not be where you are now...You owe me!"

A *parasite* is a negative, pessimistic, faithless, dreamless, and stuck in their box, dream killer who "you" have given a significant position in your life. This person shoots down all of your dreams. He or she might constantly find ways to deconstruct your destiny by pumping the fuel of negativity into your *dream engine*; causing your dreams to become stuck in park--never moving forward, but allowing time to hold you hostage. So many people who could have become famous writers, powerful ministers, successful business owners, and renowned artists find themselves crippled by the negative words of *parasites*. I've got a question for you. What types of negativity have *parasites* brought into your personal life? Did they plant negative seeds likes those listed in **Table 1** of chapter 2? If so, you need to ask God to give you the strength to *reverse the curse* of negativity that they have illegitimately placed upon you. Do yourself a grand favor and *read* scripture **Numbers 13:1-33**. I know that it is a lot of reading, but this passage will help free you from the grip of parasitic language. Please answer the following questions:

Discussion Questions

1.   What did God tell Moses to do in verse 1?

2.   What did the spies find in the land they spied out? (vv. 21-24).

3.   What did the majority of the spies say about the land of promise? (vv. 25-30).

4.   What was Caleb's response to the spies report? (vv. 30-31).

5.   What did the nation of Israel decide to do once they heard both reports? (vv. 32-33).

Some of us do not have to look far before we can identify *parasites* in our lives. You may ask, *"How does one evolve into a parasite?"* That's a great question, because *no one* is born a *parasite*. A *parasitic* mentality is shaped by *experience, time*, and *stagnation*. Did you know that "mind-sets" are transferrable from generation to generation? Like alcoholism, sexual addiction, drug use, poverty, and domestic violence, a *parasitic* mentality can be transferred by one or two ways, (a) *parental transfer* or (b) *environmental transfer*. First, let's briefly talk about *parental transfer*. The Word of God talks about the *sins of the father* transferring to future generations. For example, the *Children of Israel* were notorious for following in their fathers' footsteps. More specifically, the fathers disobeyed God by worshipping false idols. While knowing the True and living God and seeing His mighty hand deliver them from trouble and evil, these fathers were led by the popularity of worshipping their wants and own desires (I Kings 15:3). By doing this, they created an evil account in which their children could withdraw. Now, some parents have had heartache, disappointment and low-expectations in their childhood, which may have *conditioned* them to make *parasitic* comments towards their children, causing a cascading curse of *stagnation* that moves from one generation to another.

When people outside of the family impose a negative way of thinking upon a child, *environmental transfer* occurs. The circle of friends in the neighborhood, the customs, street doctrines, and a "struggle" mind-set all can become parasitic to the person who wishes to escape the grip of low-expectation, broken promises, and inferior thinking. As we get older, it is healthy to look back and ask the question, *"How did my environment shape the way I approach life, love, relationships, and goal setting?"* You will be amazed at how parallel our thinking is to our past and present environment.

Now that we've discussed *parasites*, let's briefly look at *parachutes*. According to Webster (2012), a **parachute** is *a folding, umbrella-like, fabric device with cords supporting a harness or straps for allowing a person, object, package, etc., to float down safely through the air from a great height (especially from an aircraft), rendered effective by the resistance of the air that expands it during the <u>descent</u> and* *reduces the velocity of its fall.*[2] Did you hear that? A parachute *protects* us from the elements that could otherwise harm us. Cords support our weight and allow us to reach our destination safely. Get it? A person that acts as a *parachute* will cover our dreams with motivation, protect our goals with positive feedback, and will help propel us towards our dreams that God planted in us at birth. The good thing about that is you can never have enough *parachutes* in your life. Life can bring storm showers, hail, and scorching heat, but a *parachute* can keep us afloat to safely reach our destination. I have a question for you. *Are you a parachute*? Do you build up others' dreams, or do you *tear* them down with a negative, unbelieving tongue? Think about this as you go through your day.

Pillar 7: Who Are Your Coaches?

"Michael had Phil Jackson, Peyton had Tony Dungy, and Timothy had the Apostle Paul."--Dr. Lamont Ricks

A coach is one whose *main* objective is to *develop, train, enhance, and sharpen the skills, gifts, and talents* of his or her pupils. A parachute will *support* your goals, while a coach will *develop* them. This is one prime distinction *between* a parachute and a coach. Another distinguishing factor of a coach involves their ability to *identify* a pupil's strengths and weakness. Once weaknesses are known, they are able to neutralize the weakness, while maximizing the strengths. That's right, my friend. Even the *most influential* individuals on Earth have coaches or mentors. So, what am I getting at here? Well, (1) you must *intentionally* position yourself around wise people so that your path in life can become established and prosperous and (2) you *will not* reach your destiny by yourself. You have to have key people in your life that will *pour* knowledge, understanding, and wisdom into your "dream tank."(Proverbs 15:22). The Bible is very clear on the necessity of having an *inner circle* of people who will instruct, listen, evaluate, analyze, rebuke, teach, *and* support your efforts to win at the game of life. I cannot stress how important it is to seek counsel *fervently*. Just think about this for a minute; we have *loan and debt counseling* for financial issues, *pre-marital and post-marital counseling* for marital issues, *diet and nutritional counseling* for eating issues, *pre-surgery counseling* for medical issues, and *individual counseling* for personal life issues . Why is *counseling* so critical? It is because life is full of "*domino* affect" decisions. That is, life is all about connecting the dots, so to speak. For example, questions like *who should I marry? What school should I attend? How many children should I have? What occupation or career should I choose? What church should I attend? What type of home should I purchase? How should I plan for retirement? What type of vehicle should I buy? Who should I date?* Are you getting my drift? Life is a bucket of questions that bombard us daily; therefore, we need to seek out people who can assist us with analyzing decisions from various angles. Many people have crashed in their careers, relationships, and dreams--all because they neglected to seek out wise counsel. Now, this concept may or may not be new to you, but I would like to offer a brief list of qualities that you should look for in a coach. Although the following list is a starting point, it can aid you in making wiser choices for your life:

A Good Coach will be:
- *Able to identify your weakness and your strengths*
- *Able to neutralize you weaknesses*
- *Willing to tell you the raw truth in order to help you achieve*
- *Experienced in your particular field of interest*
- *Established in the your area of interest*
- *Positive towards life*
- *One to warn you of impending danger*

- *Trustworthy*
- *Able to see what you do not see*
- *A good listener*
- *Supportive of your dreams and ambitions*
- *Honest with you*
- *Patient with you*
- *Willing to go the distance with your dream*
- *One to have Faith in you and your dream*
- *One to advise you of the pros and cons of your decisions*
- *Willing to conduct research on a matter*
- *One to challenge you to achieve at a high level*
- *One to hold you accountable in all things*
- *Helping you to block out distracting people, places, and things*

My friend, this is what *propels* you over the hump. You *must* have good coaches/counselors in your life. Coaches keep you *stabilized, level-headed,* and *hungry.* Can you imagine *all* of the praise, worship, and idolization that *Peyton Manning, Michael Jordan, Lebron James,* and *Kobe Bryant* encounter on an hourly basis? All of these men have achieved *Rock Star* status! After every game, every interview, and every moment they step out of their front doors, these sports icons are *bombarded* with sponsorship deal requests, paparazzi, professional con artists, savvy accountants, and *gorgeous* promiscuous women who are ready and willing to conduct every act of lustful pleasure under the sun. This is why many influential people need constant security, mangers, private schooling for their children, special assistants, and level-headed life *coaches* in their corners—to keep them from *crashing* into the wall of *self-indulgence, poor financial partnerships*, and *hedonism*. I would like you to read **1 Kings 12:1-19** and answer the following discussion questions.

Discussion Questions

1. Who did King Rehoboam consult with first? (vv. 6)

2. What advice did these men give to the new King? (vv. 7)

3. How did Rehoboam respond to the advice? Did he listen? (vv. 8)

4. Who did Rehoboam end up consulting with? (vv. 9-10)

5. What did the second group of counselors tell him? (vv. 11)
6. How did the people respond to Rehoboam's final decision? (vv. 16-19)

You see, we have to be extremely careful of who we choose to be in our corner when making decisions. We need to ask ourselves a big question. Are the people in my *inner* circle, *hot-headed, impulsive, selfish, gossipers,* or *parasitic*? Remember, one tends to listen to the *counsel* of those in his or her *inner circle* and only goes as far as his or her inner circle dictates. Let me ask you an honest question. Do you *own* a car or truck? If so, do you take it in for *routine* oil changes and maintenance services? If so, you are a *responsible* and *wise* owner. You understand that *irreparable damage* is done to the engine and transmission if you neglect to keep the maintenance up to date, costing you a lot of *time*, *money*, and your *sanity*--all because of *poor* planning and *refusal* to listen to *warning* signs. I've been there more than I would like to admit--and paid *dearly* for it. Sometimes we have to conduct a *routine* diagnostic analysis on our *relationships* and *partnerships* to see if everything is in working order. If you think that a *vehicle* breakdown is expensive, just imagine what a *relationship and/or partnership* breakdown will cost! This is why having coaches in our lives is so important in developing quality relationships and securing personal success. No man or woman is an island. Anyone worth his or her weight in salt had some form of assistance to arrive to the level of success he or she now enjoys. All you have to do is pay attention to the *warning* signs. Now do you see the importance of having coaches? Take this time to analyze your inner circle of friends. Do you need to reposition some people? If so, ask God to give you wisdom and guidance on how to do so.

Pillar 8: Mind-Set Breeds Material Rewards

" When you believe in what you do, people will believe in you, and people will believe you. And this is the life-blood of confidence in self."--Dr. Lamont Ricks

I want to talk about the word, *collateral*. Now, what does *collateral* mean? According to Webster (2012), **Collateral** is *security pledged for the payment of a loan. Security* is another word for *something* that you own or possess[1]; say a stock, property, jewels, or antique glass. When a person takes out a loan for an amount of money that is *beyond* their current income, the bank or lending agency may ask for *collateral*. That is, they want some form of repayment, should a person default on their loan. Think about it, the bank is taking a huge *risk* on you based on one thing, your word. However, the banks are not that naïve. The underlying understanding is this, *"If you don't pay back this loan, we will take what you already own, that is, physical collateral"*. It is my belief that the *mind* allows us to create collateral. We will call this *Intellectual collateral*. That is, the *thoughts* of a man can produce physical rewards of his labor. Let me render an example of what I am asserting here. Tyler Perry is a famous playwright, producer, director, actor, and author. He is best known for his role as *Madea, a fictional character he created in his mind* (intellectual collateral). Before

Mr. Perry became a household name, he began to promote his stage plays at the 14th Street Playhouse in Atlanta, GA. It took him over 6 years for audiences to take notice of his skill. Many of his plays had poor showings. He would use every cent of his tax return checks to help fund his plays-*all to no avail*. No matter how dismal the showing, he never lost confidence, but increased in confidence all the more. Why? because he never stopped believing in his dream. One day, after 6 years of setbacks, he finally got his big break. He utilized local preachers and pastors to perform in his plays. His hard work resulted in a sold out weekend. This was the beginning of something BIG!!! His plays earned him so much media fanfare that he garnered enough money (physical collateral) to transform them into Hollywood blockbusters. At first, all of the Hollywood production companies rejected him, but he didn't let that stop him from following his dream. Now, Mr. Perry earns in excess of $100 million per year in salary (www.forbes.com)! Talk about material rewards (physical collateral)! You see, Tyler Perry knew something that many people, including myself, often overlook. He *created* his own success. He took an idea out of his mind and gave it *shoes*. That is, He didn't let his dreams die in his mind, but allowed them to spill over into his actions. This reflects one important theme I want you to remember: *Create your own success, with God's help of course. What are some of the dreams you let die because you were too afraid of being laughed at or rejected? What business ideas or inventions did God place in your brain, only to have it fizzle out by doubt? Do you know that everything we see, use, purchase, sell, and eat was first an idea in someone's mind?* Those who have acquired success merely took the risk of putting *shoes* on their dreams and ran with it! Once a person secures physical collateral, they can create more *opportunities* for themselves. We are in a constant state of building intellectual or physical collateral throughout our life-span. Regardless of age, gender, or background, the person who has established some form of collateral has more bargaining power, which translates into more *options* in this life.

A person's mind-set can direct him or her down the road of poverty or great wealth. It's all about your mind-set. As a man thinks, so is he (Proverbs 23:7a). You will find that many people who have found a measure of fulfillment in their lives have a treasure trove of *intellectual* collateral bubbling under their skin and this wellspring of ideas will translate into a *multitude of options*. This is what transformed Tyler Perry from a homeless man to a household name-his MIND-SET. What kind of mind-set do you have? If you can think it, you can become it.

Now, you may ask, how does one *create* collateral? Well, let's look, for example, at the job application process. First, you have to *possess* the qualifications for the job in which you are interested. If you do not have the qualifications, you must *find out* how you can become qualified. Maybe you need to take an additional class, build upon your résumé or vita, network with people in the field, earn a particular degree, or enroll in a qualifying certification course. Second, you must *believe* in your *abilities* and your *aptitude*. An *ability* is a skill in which you can accomplish a task under *normal* circumstances. *Aptitudes* are *potential* abilities that will come with time in order to accomplish future tasks, if provided the requisite resources. This is how higher learning institutions and Military agencies sift through the sea of applicants. They want to know if you have the *ability* and the *aptitude* to not only *enroll* into their organization, but the *wherewithal, dogged perseverance, knowledge base, skill-set, potential,* and *mindset* to *complete* the training and education afforded by their organization successfully. Third, you must be able to *persuade* people with your abilities and aptitudes by effectively *communicating* your *worth* to the hiring managers of the company where you wish to work . Fourth, you have to *believe in God's* mighty hand, *not* your own strength as the *game changer* in the decision of those who will give you that particular job or opportunity. Finally, you must believe the battle is already won; you simply have to catch up to what is going to happen in your life--*and this takes faith* (Hebrews 11:1 and 6).

God and Your Collateral

The key to lasting spiritual fulfillment is to simply *know* who God is. Take a look at the following Biblical scripture and think about the prophet Jeremiah's words as it relates to your personal life. When we fully understand that God is the judge of the living and the dead, the King of Glory, and the ultimate

Master of our life, we will approach problems in a healthy fashion.

Jeremiah 9: 23-24 states:

> "23 Thus says the LORD, " Let not a wise man boast of his wisdom, and let not the mighty man boast of his might, let not a rich man boast of his riches; 24 but let him who boasts boast of this, that he understands and knows Me, that I am the LORD who exercises loving kindness, justice and righteousness on earth; for I delight in these things," declares the LORD." (NASB).

King David of the Bible is a perfect example of a person who *knew* and *understood* God *and* had confidence in his *own* abilities and aptitude. Many of us know how this story goes. Although God can do *anything* in our personal lives, He *will not* do everything for us. We have to bring *intellectual collateral* (i.e. an overcomer's mind-set) to the table that He can use for His Glory! David certainly did this very thing. I want you to look at the passage below and see how David had confidence in God, which gave birth to *physical collateral*. David's confidence was so high that it persuaded King Saul to approve him for battle against the Philistine giant named Goliath.

In **1 Samuel 17: 34-37** it powerfully states the following:

> "34 But David said to Saul, "Your servant was tending his father's sheep. When a lion or a bear came and took a lamb from the flock, 35 I went out after him and attacked him, and rescued it from his mouth; and when he rose up against me, I seized him by his beard and struck him and killed him. 36 Your servant has killed both the lion and the bear; and this uncircumcised Philistine will be like one of them, since he has taunted the armies of the living God."

37 And David said, " The LORD who delivered me from the paw of the lion and from the paw of the bear, He will deliver me from the hand of this Philistine." And Saul said to David, "Go, and may the LORD be with you." (NASB)

David possessed *intellectual* and *physical* collateral like no other character in the Bible. Just think about it; a lion *and* a bear are very big, strong, fast, fearless, and ferocious carnivores (man eaters). A lion can reach speeds up to 50 miles per hour. A bear can run up to speeds of 35 mph. Now you may say, "that's fast, but not *that* fast". Oh really? Well the fastest human recorded has reached the speed of 23 to 25 mph. Do you see my point now? In addition, we must remember that David was a *boy*. A young teenager at the time he accomplished the *impossible* (killing the lion, bear, *and* Goliath). I like what David said in verse 35. He said, *"I went after the lion and the bear."* Do you understand what He is saying here? Listen, sometimes the *blessings of God* are clutched in the mouths of lions and bears. God wants us to have the *courage* to attack the *giants* in our lives in order to get what *already* belongs to us! David used the *victories of his past* to reclaim the present prize of destroying the giant that was standing in the way of his destiny of becoming the greatest King of Israel! What a *beautiful* and *powerful* principle! Are there *giants* in your life that have been standing in the way of you becoming the queen or king of your God-given blessing? Is it a person with a *parasitic* mindset who wants to drain the life out of you for their own personal gain? Is it a person with a *chicken mentality* who tries to limit you because of their own fear? Is it the *shackles* of low self-esteem and depression? Is it your own insecurities? Is it your abusive father or mother's voice in your head? What is it? Whatever name you give it, you and God *know* that it is a *giant* in your life, trying to feed your *destiny* to the birds of *oblivion*. I'm here to tell you to *rise* up in the *name of Jesus* and *attack* that *giant* that has immobilized you with *fear, doubt,* and *hopelessness* and in God's name, get your REWARDS!

Discussion Questions

1. Based on **1 Samuel 17** (whole chapter) what can we assume about David?

2. How did David's brothers respond to him when he decided to fight Goliath? (vv. 26-29)

3. What should we do when faced with a giant in our lives? (vv. 34-37)

4. Who is the true source of our power to destroy the giants in our lives? (vv. 37)

Pillar 9: Get to Know The TRUTH

"Truth doesn't always make a lot of noise, but it can be heard loud and clear."--Dr. Lamont Ricks

Why is *Truth* so important? Well, the *Truth* is the precise standard by which all reality of a situation is hinged. To me, that is the only characteristic of truth that distinguishes it from falsehood. Simply put, truth is what "really" is. It is as simple as that. The powerful fact about Truth is it (1) stands alone, (2) is not changed by time, and (3) Is an instrument of deliverance. Truth is like a mirror; it shows a person what they really look like. For example, you wake up every morning and go to the restroom to bathe, prepare your clothes for the day, and look at yourself. You look to see what is really going on physically. Figuratively speaking, we have many representations of *Truth* in our society, via vocational fields. We go to the doctor to hear the truth about our health. We go to the mechanic to hear the truth about our cars (well, the honest mechanics). We go to the dentist to hear the truth about our teeth and gums. We go to the tax person to hear and see the truth about our fiscal spending. You see, the aforementioned professions have "instruments" that reveal what's "really" going on with us. I don't care how good you may feel, how fast you may run, or how strong your muscles are, the doctor can test your blood and find diseases within your "so-called" healthy body that can damage your health down the road. That is, s/he can find the "precise standard" on which reality (your health) is hinged upon. The Word of God is the Truth. Second **Timothy 3:16** states the following:

> "All Scripture is inspired by God and profitable for teaching, for reproof, for correction, for training in righteousness;" (NASB)

In **John 17:13-19**, Jesus made the following declaration and request to God the Father in His prayer for His Disciples:

> "13 But now I come to you; and these things I speak in the world so that they may have My joy made full in themselves. 14 I have given them Your word; and the world has hated them, because they are not of the world, even as I am not of the world. 15 I do not ask You to take them out of the world, but to keep them from the evil one. 16 They are not of the world, even as I am not of the world. 17 Sanctify them in the truth; Your word is truth. 18 As You sent Me into the world, I also have sent them into the world. 19 For their sakes I sanctify Myself, that they themselves also may be sanctified in truth." (NASB).

Did you hear that? Jesus said that the *Word*, that is, the *Scriptures* is truth. What a liberating statement that we can trust. Notice, He didn't say your Word "*contains*" the truth, or "*resembles*" the truth, or "*points*" to the truth. He *clearly* says that the Word *is* Truth. This is a *juggernaut* fact that the Bible *is* truth! This is why we can put our lives on the Word of God. This is why so many people have given their lives for the Word on mission fields, war zones, and in the ministry. Although the secular world may not admit it, they still *confirm* that the Word of God *is* Truth. When a President is inaugurated (sworn in) he places his hand on what? *The Bible.* The institution of heterosexual marriage is based upon what? *The Bible.* When you stay at a hotel, what do you find in the nightstand? *The Bible.* When you visit the hospital waiting room, particularly ICU (Intensive Care Unit), what do you see near the magazines? *The Bible.* Even the media, which is heavily influenced by the spirit of sensationalism, sensuality, gossip, and motivated by scandal, describes devastating events, such as Hurricanes, Floods, Earthquakes, and other major events as *Biblical proportions.* You see, even *secular* organizations vicariously *recognize* the *Truth,* but it is supremely important that we understand *recognition* does not equate to *acceptance* and *obedience.* For example, if you are speeding down the highway, you are (in reality) *breaking the law* and un-equivocally *earned* the *consequences* of breaking that particular law (i.e., a speeding ticket). Now, if you are like me you would say, I was in a hurry, or I was running late for a very important appointment (which *may* be correct). However, the truth is that I was still *breaking the law.* Are you ready for this? If I am a lawbreaker, then I can also be identified as having law breaking tendencies. When I speed, I have to come to grips with that logic; for in that moment, I entered an atmosphere of *crime.* This is why *confession* of sin is so important. Every day, we involve ourselves in some form or level of *sin,* whether it's as simple as a pen, some copy paper, or time we may have stolen from the office. Whatever it may be, we have to ask God to *forgive* us daily. Now you might be thinking, "Dr. Ricks, you are going too far. That is so petty. I'm a good person, and I don't bother anybody! How dare you!"

My friend, I didn't tell you the Truth *always* felt good; sometimes it stings like a hornet. Hey, this hit me between the eyes too, and honestly, I was a bit *taken aback* by the thought that I had *law breaking tendencies* before a Holy God, but I had to *accept* the *Truth*. Therefore, so do you, my friend. Do you see how Truth doesn't care what your reasons are? Truth shows us who we "really" are. Let's look at Romans 3:9-18; 23.

> *"What then? Are we better than they? Not at all; for we have already charged that both Jews and Greeks are all under sin;* [10] *as it is written," THERE IS NONE RIGHTEOUS, NOT EVEN ONE;*[11] *THERE IS NONE WHO UNDERSTANDS, THERE IS NONE WHO SEEKS FOR GOD;*[12] *ALL HAVE TURNED ASIDE, TOGETHER THEY HAVE BECOME USELESS; THERE IS NONE WHO DOES GOOD, THERE IS NOT EVEN ONE."*[13] *" THEIR THROAT IS AN OPEN GRAVE, WITH THEIR TONGUES THEY KEEP DECEIVING,"" THE POISON OF ASPS IS UNDER THEIR LIPS";*[14] *" WHOSE MOUTH IS FULL OF CURSING AND BITTERNESS";*[15] *" THEIR FEET ARE SWIFT TO SHED BLOOD,*[16] *DESTRUCTION AND MISERY ARE IN THEIR PATHS,*[17] *AND THE PATH OF PEACE THEY HAVE NOT KNOWN."*[18] *" THERE IS NO FEAR OF GOD BEFORE THEIR EYES."*[23] *for all have sinned and fall short of the glory of God,"* (NASB)

According to the above text you've just read, all mankind are *law break*ers, *full of death, sin, deceit, murder, lies, lust, slander, or scandal*, etc. Bottom line is none of our hands are clean; not mine, not yours. Nevertheless, there is good news.

Jesus came to emancipate us from the slave market of sin and death by dying on a rugged cross, and resurrecting from the dead. My friend, if you are reading this and you have *never* trusted your soul to Christ, you are really a *dead* man or *dead* woman walking; living on *borrowed* time. Give your life over to Jesus Christ before it is too late. This may be the first *and* last time you hear the message of the *Cross*. You may die tonight in a car accident, in your sleep, at a party, or at work. *No one* knows when death is coming for, but I can assure you of this, you *will* live again. However, you will live in one of two places, *Heaven* or *Hell*. Whether you agree with me or not, I hope I've got your attention.

Salvation Prayer

"Dear God, based upon what I've read I acknowledge that I am a sinner (law breaker) and that I cannot save myself from this condition. I believe that Jesus Christ died on the cross for my sins, was buried in a tomb and resurrected from the dead, and today, I ask that Jesus Christ come into my heart to live eternally. Save me from your eternal wrath. In Jesus name, Amen."

If you prayed a prayer like this and you *really* meant it from your heart, welcome to the Family of God! You have just removed your name from hotel Hell's registry. You have just received the Holy Spirit Who will live and abide with you in the good times and the bad times; when you are living right and when you falter. Below, I've listed a few Scriptures that describe your salvation from the slave market of sin. Please read them daily until God gives you a full understanding.

John 5: 24 states,

> *"Truly, truly, I say to you, he who hears My word, and believes Him who sent Me, has eternal life, and does not come into judgment, but has passed out of death into life."* (NASB)

Romans 10:9 says,

> *"⁹that if you confess with your mouth Jesus as Lord, and believe in your heart that God raised Him from the dead, you will be saved; ¹⁰for with the heart a person believes, resulting in righteousness, and with the mouth he confesses, resulting in salvation."* (NASB)

Jesus Christ is so powerful that the Bible states the following in

Colossians 1:13-20:

> *"¹³For He rescued us from the domain of darkness, and transferred us to the kingdom of His beloved Son, ¹⁴ in whom we have redemption, the forgiveness of sins.¹⁵ He is the image of the invisible God, the firstborn of all creation. ¹⁶ For by Him all things were created, both in the heavens and on earth, visible and invisible, whether thrones or dominions or rulers or authorities— all things have been created through Him and for Him. ¹⁷ He is before all things, and in Him all things hold together. ¹⁸ He is also head of the body, the church; and He is the beginning, the firstborn from the dead, so that He Himself will come to have first place in everything. ¹⁹ For it was the Father's good pleasure for all the fullness to dwell in Him, ²⁰ and through Him to reconcile all things to Himself, having made peace through the blood of His cross; through Him, I say, whether things on earth or things in heaven."* (NASB).

John 3:3-7 declares the following:

> *"3 Jesus answered and said to him, "Truly, truly, I say to you, unless one is born again he cannot see the kingdom of God."4 Nicodemus said to Him, "How can a man be born when he is old? He cannot enter a second time into his mother's womb and be born, can he?" 5 Jesus answered, "Truly, truly, I say to you, unless one is born of water and the Spirit he cannot enter into the kingdom of God. 6 That which is born of the flesh is flesh, and that which is born of the Spirit is spirit. 7 Do not be amazed that I said to you, 'You must be born again."* (NASB)

Colossians 1:21-23 triumphantly boasts the following:

> *"21 And although you were formerly alienated and hostile in mind, engaged in evil deeds, 22 yet He has now reconciled you in His fleshly body through death, in order to present you before Him holy and blameless and beyond reproach— 23 if indeed you continue in the faith firmly established and steadfast, and not moved away from the hope of the gospel that you have heard, which was proclaimed in all creation under heaven, and of which I, Paul, was made a minister."* (NASB)

What Now, Dr. Ricks?

If you do not have a Bible, go to the local Christian Bookstore (e.g. Family Book Store, Heaven and Earth, ScriptureTruth.com, etc.) and ask the sales associate that you need a good study Bible with notes, concordance, and commentary (e.g. a New Kings James Version, NIV, or New American Standard Version, or ESV version).

1. Check out *www.oneplace.com* for good solid Christian preaching and teaching. This does not replace going to Church, but supplements your spiritual growth during the week.
2. Find a good Church that preaches the Bible. You do not have to join right away. There are many great churches that will fit your spiritual, social, and cultural needs. When you find a good Church, let the leader know that you have just received Jesus Christ as your savior.
3. Pray every night and every morning when you wake up. Get in the habit of giving God glory and thanks for saving you and loving you more than life itself.
4. Grow in the Word of God by reading your new Bible every day. A great place to start is the Book of Psalms.
5. Remember that growing takes a lot of time. Don't get frustrated when life sometimes throw you setbacks...Just get back up and start back on the right road (Proverbs 24:16)

That is the TRUTH. Be blessed, my friend.

Pillar 10: Better vs. Bitter

"Half-empty or Half-full, you make the call."--Dr. Lamont Ricks

When I was in college, I took a few courses in Psychology. In Psychology 101, I learned that a person could look at life as a glass of water. If you have a glass of water that is half-filled, you could look at it as either half-empty or half-full. That is, you can look at a situation as an *obstacle* to defeat you or an *opportunity* to promote you. I infer that this is the distinction between an *attitude of success* and an *attitude of failure*. You see, what I'm asserting here is not rocket science. This is a tried and true principle. In this life, you *will* face *uncertainty, heartache, closed doors, frustration, and unbelief.* But the *key* is how you view the "overall" message of your "temporary" misery. Today, I want to leave you with a comforting passage and a powerful story of a man who faced "un-deserved" crimes against him. First, let's start with the passage, **Romans 8:26-28** which states,

> *"26 In the same way the Spirit also helps our weakness; for we do not know how to pray as we should, but the Spirit Himself intercedes for us with groanings too deep for words; 27 and He who searches the hearts knows what the mind of the Spirit is, because He intercedes for the saints according to the will of God.28 And we know that God causes all things to work together for good to those who*

love God, to those who are called according to His purpose." (NASB).

This is a very powerful passage, particularly if you are going through a trying time, are afflicted, or tormented by *unexpected* circumstances. God has equipped every *believer* with the Holy Spirit. The Bible teaches that the Holy Spirit is the same essence as God, therefore He *is* God. The Holy Spirit lives, or abides in each believer in Christ. His main job is to *comfort, convict,* and *convert* man. When we sin against God, the Holy Spirit (along with our conscience) sends off the alarm that we have done wrong and we are in a danger zone. Sometimes, we can become so engrossed into a trial that we cannot even find the words to pray. There seems to be a fog and life stands still in a swampy, convoluted, muck. I've been there a time or two. All it takes is the right "blind-side" hit and you are thrust into a spiritual concussion. But there is hope! The Holy Spirit will pray for us. The Holy Spirit *knows* the mind of God and He knows the mindset we are in; therefore, we can be confident that God will hear our cry and deliver in "His" time and in "His" way.

I would like for you to focus your attention on verse 28. This states that God *causes* all things to work together *for* good to those who *love* God, etc. Now, you may say, I have had a lot of nasty things happen to me in my past. How in the world can I say those things were *good*?! Well, let's take a serious look at the wording here. The verse says God "causes" all things (including the things that have scarred your self-image, self-esteem, and self-confidence) to work *together* for the "overall" good of the person who loves God. He did not say that all things that happen to us *are* good. We live in a fallen world; therefore, it is impossible for everything in this life to be good *all of the time*. A condition is mentioned here. An individual is identified as *"loving"* God. This means that there is a *close relationship* between the person and God. Think of it as cooking *baked fish* in a *hot* oven. When I bake fish, I usually use pepper, salt, lemons, green peppers, and onions. Now, a lemon has a "sour" taste and will make you frown, lemon pepper will make you sneeze *uncontrollably*, salt can send a shocking tinge through your taste buds, and we all know onions *burn* your eyes and cause you to cry. Green peppers have a *bitter* taste. But the beauty of it all being cooked *together* is that when it comes out of the oven, it is some of the best tasting healthy food you can eat. Do you see what I'm saying? God is the chef and we are the fish and sometimes we will be placed in the "oven" of life, causing us pain, agony, depression, and confusion. When we encounter God in a loving and personal way, He will "force" the lemons of our past and the onions of our hurts to season our life to a point where people will want to take a bite out of our lives. We can look back over the precipice of time and say, "although that person or situation caused unbelievable pain, God's love ran deeper than my pain and my story can breathe life in others who may feel *hopeless*." This is where Romans 8:28 becomes alive!

At this time, I would like us to look at a Joseph, a man who had *every* reason to go off, lose his mind, and lose his faith. In the Book of Genesis chapters 37 through 42, we see this man's life shaped by both *good* and *bad* situations. This young man was one of the youngest of several children. His father Jacob really loved him above his siblings. Jacob placed so much favor on Joseph that he had a coat of many colors hand-made for him. Now, this wasn't some Halloween costume, but a beautifully ornate piece of fabric that represented great value. Of course, this outward show of love infuriated Joseph's brothers to the point that they wanted to kill him. To make matters worse, Joseph frequently shared his vision of being the best of his brothers. Now, if you know anything about being an older sibling that is not going to set well with you. Talk about sibling rivalry. It's one thing when one brother is mad at you, but to have 10 older brothers ticked off at you is *not* good at all. So, they came up with a dastardly plan; kill Joseph, take his coat of many colors, place the blood of an animal on the coat, and tell dad that a beast had slaughtered his beloved son. Well, three fourths of the plan was carried out, except for the "killing" part. They beat Joseph, threw him into a pit and decided to sell Joseph to the slave market. Can you believe the audacity of these blood brothers? I tell you, that is what jealousy is capable of doing. It is a *nasty, unforgiving* phenomenon, rooted in an abnormal vein of competition. Once Joseph was sold into slavery, he landed a servant's position with Potiphar, an Egyptian Executioner. As Potiphar's slave, Joseph was given several responsibilities, including looking after Potiphar's home. The Bible says that the Lord was with Joseph; therefore, he found great favor with Potiphar and moved up in the realm of responsibility. Joseph was making what we may call today, power moves--even as a slave! Unfortunately, things took a turn for the worst. The Bible states Joseph was handsome in form and appearance. Let's break that down in today's terms. The man was good looking. Ladies, my man Joseph, looked like a *Brad Pitt* or a *young Denzel Washington* or *Idris Elba* or whoever you think looks fine and well built. My point is, he made the ladies drool at the sight of his Hebrew physique. Moreover, there was one woman in particular who was caught up by Joseph's good looks, *Mrs. Potiphar.* That right, His slave master's wife! Not only was she *caught up*, she *spoke up,* and *turned up the heat*--in a provocative manner! The Bible clearly says that on "several" occasions she would approach Joseph and ask if she could have sex with him. That's right, it's in the Bible. I would contend that this was the first documented case of *sexual harassment* on the job. Can you imagine how awkward this must have been for, Joseph? Think about it. You are a slave, meaning that you have no voice, no rights, and you are a piece of property and someone wants to force you to do something *against* your will. This can be very painful and emotionally scar a person for life. But Joseph, being a man of God, *resisted* the temptation to have sexual relations with this woman and made two very important declarative statements: (1) *"How can I sin against my God by doing this* and (2) *Your husband has entrusted everything in this house except for you, for you are his wife!"* Good for Joseph, right? Wrong!

Although Joseph took a powerful stand for God by resisting this woman's advances, the Bible says that on a particular day when no one else was around, Potiphar's wife grabbed Joseph by the coat and *demanded* that he have sex with her. Joseph did what any *God fearing* man *should* do, run, run, run! He didn't say he would fast and pray over it, he didn't call up his accountability partner, he didn't argue with this woman, he simply got out of dodge! You see, my friend, there are some vices, temptations, and even people in your life that you *can't* be alone with, or you may give in to their desires to have you. You have to understand this one thing: when someone keeps *badgering* you there are two ways to respond, (1) you could get so weak that you yield to their wishes or (2) get your wits about you and *flee* the scene. Joseph did the latter. The Bible further states that she lied and accused him of attempted rape. This news made Potiphar very, very angry causing Joseph to be thrown into prison. But God was with Joseph. Even in prison, Joseph found favor with the prison warden, inmates, and guards. My friend, when God is ordering your steps, you will win, *even* in losing circumstances. Notice, God did not *deliver* Joseph *"out"* of prison; He delivered him *"through"* the prison. You see, *deliverance* comes in many shapes, sizes, and styles. Don't get me wrong, I am the type of person who "always" prefers to be delivered "out" of a storm, not through it (Mark 4:35-41). But God "knows" what we need more than we know. His thoughts are not like our thoughts, nor are His ways like our ways (Isaiah 55:8-9).

After spending several *years* in prison, God gave Joseph a *special gift* of interpreting the dreams of others. There were two people, in particular, whose dreams he interpreted on the same day, a *Baker* and a *Cupbearer*. The Cupbearer was an official in Pharaoh's palace that tasted his drinks to see if they were poisoned. His job was very dangerous and he only had one shot to get it wrong or he would die on the spot. The Cupbearer had a dream about three branches and ripe grapes being squeezed into the Pharaoh's cup. *Joseph's interpretation*: In three days, the Cupbearer would be re-instated to his previous position with the King. Joseph, being a wise man, asked the Cupbearer to "drop his name" on the Pharaoh. Joseph was *getting real* about his situation with the Cupbearer. In today's terminology Joseph said,

> *"Look man, please, please, please put in a good word for me to   Pharaoh. I don't want to be here in his cesspool of a prison. I've been sold into slavery and framed by a lying*

witch of a woman! I've done no wrong! Don't forget about me, man!"

I like this statement that Joseph made because it shows the *authenticity* of his faith and character. Some people *rejoice* in their suffering, making *unrealistic, hyper-spiritual* comments, like. *"I'm thankful I'm sick," or "I enjoy my illness," or "Money doesn't mean anything to me, so I'm content with being broke as Joe's Turkey."* In **Second Corinthians 12:7-10**, it powerfully renders the following:

> *"7 Because of the surpassing greatness of the revelations, for this reason, to keep me from exalting myself, there was given me a thorn in the flesh, a messenger of Satan to torment me—to keep me from exalting myself! 8 Concerning this I implored the Lord three times that it might leave me. 9 And He has said to me, "My grace is sufficient for you, for power is perfected in weakness." Most gladly, therefore, I will rather boast about my weaknesses, so that the power of Christ may dwell in me. 10 Therefore I am well content with weaknesses, with insults, with distresses, with persecutions, with difficulties, for Christ's sake; for when I am weak, then I am strong."* (NASB)

Can I be transparent, here? The Apostle Paul had a physical ailment or problem that agitated his body to no end. He called this physical ailment a *thorn in the flesh*. Have you ever had a speck of sand in your eye or a splinter in your finger? It can be quite uncomfortable to say the least. What a relief when you remove that splinter or sand particle. Well, Paul did not have this luxury of relief. He *asked* God on *three* separate occasions to remove this *physical* ailment from his body. However, God's answer was a resounding, "No! My *grace* will be made perfect in your weaknesses". Notice, Paul made a decision to boast in God's power *through* his ailment (weaknesses). Basically, he wasn't going to get *down on himself* because God didn't give him what he desired (healing), he was going to use his ailment as a powerful *Billboard* of God's sustaining power! You see, the joy was *not* specifically *in* his weakness, it was in his *faith* in a *powerful*, *loving* God working through him despite his weakness! If the Apostle Paul thought it was a *joy*, so to speak, to have this *unknown physical ailment*, he would *not* have asked God to *remove* it on *three separate occasions*.

All of these comments are *misinformed* statements based on the *false* pretense of *religiosity*. The Pharisees were *no* different. Although they bragged about their *religious* rituals, prayers, fasting, tithing, and deep knowledge of the Law of God, their *hearts* were *not* with God at all. So too, are the *genuine* Christians who assert that struggle *enhances* their *spirituality* and *sanctification*. It surely does not. Some Christians actually believe that being *poor* equates to having a closer relationship with God, or that being ill *all of the time* equals a higher rank in the Heavenly realms. This thought process couldn't be further from the truth! The bottom line is this: Rich people go to heaven *and* poor people go to heaven; Rich people go to Hell *and* poor people go to Hell. Healthy people go to heaven *and* sickly people go to heaven; Healthy people go to Hell as well as sickly people. What *determines* your eternal destination is *not* your *socio-economic status* or your *health status*, but your *soul-status*. Receiving Jesus Christ as your Lord and Savior *is* the determinant factor, *not* any *man-made* categorical class-status indicators. I hope I *freed* somebody right there. Now the Bible clearly teaches that any *follower* of God *will suffer* persecution and that we should be *content* in *whatsoever* state we find ourselves. However, we *should* rejoice in the *Lord*, *not* our situation or condition. Additionally, we should *use* our situation or condition as a ministerial tool to witness to the lost. This validates that our rejoicing is in the *Lord*, not our illness, weakness, poverty, or setback, but the *Lord*. I cannot express this fact enough. So many *well-meaning* Christians who genuinely love God are trapped in this man-made bondage of a *suffering theology*. We should be *content* that we *know* the "LORD", not the trials of our *specific* circumstances. That is the *distinction*. What *fool* prays that s/he goes to jail? What *sane* person prays that they will develop cancer, HIV, MS, Diabetes, Lupus, or Cystic Fibrosis? What *intelligent* individual prays for un-employment or underemployment, in which they cannot feed their children? What person prays that they be involved in a tragic car accident? NO ONE! Sometimes God allows *tragedy* to ride *"shot-gun"* in the passenger seat of our lives in order to get us to *lock* our sights and minds on the Lord and His promises, His provision, and His power. In essence, God wants us to be *solely dependent* upon Him. Therefore, He will "use" *traumatic situations* to catalyze praise, prayer, and worship from our lips. This is what **2 Corinthians 12:7-10** was all about. Now let's get back to my friend, Joseph.

Although the Cupbearer received a good report from Joseph, The Baker's dream did not render favorable results. He dreamed that he had a basket of food on his head and the birds came and lifted the food from off his head. *Joseph's Interpretation*: Joseph stated that in a three days, the executioner would lift (cut off) the Baker's head from his body and that the birds would eat the flesh of his hanging corpse. The dream came true! The Cupbearer, just as Joseph prophesied, did get his position back with the King, but he totally forgot about Joseph, thus Joseph was left to rot in that Egyptian jail for two more years--*all because his brothers sold him out and Potiphar's wife framed him.* But the story is far from over. One day the Pharaoh had a terrible nightmare about his kingdom. In his dream, he saw seven fat ears of corn and seven dried up ears of corn. The dried up, disease ridden ears of corn *consumed* the seven fat and healthy ears of corn. He also saw a vision of seven fat cows and seven malnourished cows and just like the corn, the seven malnourished cows devoured the seven healthy cows. He was so *terrified* by the dream, that he sought out the *best minds* in all the kingdom to help him interpret this nightmare. No wise man could come close to understanding what the

dream meant. It was at this divinely appointed moment that the
Cupbearer was reminded about Joseph's plea for help and his
power to interpret dreams. Pharaoh rushed Joseph out of
prison, shaved his head, and cleaned him up so he would be
presentable. Pharaoh asked Joseph to interpret the dream.
Joseph, once again being a man of deep faith, gave the glory to
God for being able to interpret Pharaoh's dream. *Joseph's
interpretation*: You will have seven years of plenty and seven
years of famine! Store up food and resources during your years
of plenty and you will be spared during the seven years of lean
times. Pharaoh was comforted and in awe of Joseph's skill at
dream interpretation. God gave Joseph such descriptive power
that Pharaoh not only released Joseph out of prison, he
promoted Joseph to *second* in command over the *entire* Egyptian
realm--all because Joseph was faithful to God under tremendous
stress, uncertainty, lies, and betrayal. In all, Joseph spent
approximately 12-13 years in prison. Now that's a long time.
What was it that kept Joseph's faith strong in God? I can tell you
this; Joseph's relationship with God was PERSONAL and REAL.
God never left Joseph.

As the 7 years of plenty subsided, famine struck the
world with an insatiable fury. Countries that bordered Egypt
needed dire assistance with resources, most notably, food. We
must remember, Joseph had 11 brothers and other family
members back home. The famine was relentless. It did not show

anyone any mercy. Nonetheless, God's mighty hand used Joseph to establish the kingdom of Egypt. It came time for Jacob to send his sons to Egypt to request food and resources. Not knowing that Joseph was in Egypt, the brothers set off to request assistance. When they got there, Joseph immediately recognized them, but they did not recognize Joseph, so he did not reveal that he was their long lost brother. He asked them if they could bring their youngest brother to Egypt. The brothers were confused, but they went back and requested that the youngest, Benjamin, return to Egypt. Reluctantly, Jacob agreed. After playing a few mind games on his older brothers, Joseph cried bitterly, a genuine case of catharsis. Just imagine, these guys were *completely* responsible for his slavery, being set up by Potiphar's wife, and spending 13 years of his *innocent* life in prison, doing hard time! Only God can give a human being the *restraint* that Joseph exhibited. As he got himself together, he *revealed* his true heritage. This is the kicker! Although Joseph could have had each of his older brothers executed in the streets, he made a *prolific* statement. He said, "what you did to me, you meant for *evil*, but it was God who meant it all for *good!*" In all of this, God said that he was with Joseph. You see the *presence* of God doesn't always equate to the *intervention of God* or *deliverance of God*. Many times, we assume that God does not love us because He allowed horrible and unspeakable things to happen to us. Some of us may have suffered verbal, physical, or sexual abuse in our childhood. Some of us may have been mistreated or wrongfully accused. Some of us may have been victims of a heinous crime. Some of us may have been terminated from our job, without a justifiable cause. Regardless of the circumstance, we can now rest in knowing that God "will" work it all out *for* our good. Joseph went from the *slave house* to the *jail house;* from the *prison* to the *palace. Only God* can do that! Give Him the Glory! You see, you *never* forget the people who have hurt or scarred you in your life, but you can *forgive* them. Glory to God! Joseph decided to become *better* instead of becoming *bitter*! Remember, the pain you experienced in your past does not have the final say in whether you become bitter or better. Don't allow a lie to become your truth. God is more than able to turn your lemons of life into sweet lemonade.

Pillar 11: Obstacles vs. Opportunity

"Then Caleb quieted the people before Moses and said, "We should by all means go up and take possession of it, for we will surely overcome it."--Numbers 13:30 (NASB)

What are obstacles? Well let's just say an obstacle is an obstruction that gets in the way of a desired result. Say a foreign object gets jammed into your eye. Man that hurts! Your eyes quickly become red because of the irritants and you tear up in an effort to wash the object out of your eye. Now why does the eye automatically react this way? Simple, the foreign object is not supposed to be there. It has made itself an obstacle, but there is an opportunity to relieve yourself of the pain built into the obstacle that is causing you pain. Check out the following dialogue in Numbers 13:25-33 to see how two vantage points play out.

The Spies' Analyses

> *"25 When they returned from spying out the land, at the end of forty days, 26 they proceeded to come to Moses and Aaron and to all the congregation of the sons of Israel in the wilderness of Paran, at Kadesh; and they brought back word to them and to all the congregation and showed them the fruit of the land. 27 Thus they told him, and said, "We went in to the land where you sent us; and it certainly does flow with milk and honey, and this is its fruit. 28 Nevertheless, the people who live in the land are strong,*

and the cities are fortified and very large; and moreover, we saw the descendants of Anak there. 29 Amalek is living in the land of the Negev and the Hittites and the Jebusites and the Amorites are living in the hill country, and the Canaanites are living by the sea and by the side of the Jordan.30 Then Caleb quieted the people before Moses and said, "We should by all means go up and take possession of it, for we will surely overcome it." 31 But the men who had gone up with him said, " We are not able to go up against the people, for they are too strong for us." 32 So they gave out to the sons of Israel a bad report of the land which they had spied out, saying, "The land through which we have gone, in spying it out, is a land that devours its inhabitants; and all the people whom we saw in it are men of great size. 33 There also we saw the Nephilim (the sons of Anak are part of the Nephilim); and we became like grasshoppers in our own sight, and so we were in their sight." (NASB)

Intimidation is a terrible phenomenon. It can immobilize you from walking through a door that God has already confirmed in your heart. Suppose, you are at a job where you face injustices. Your boss gives you a hard time, nitpicks every little thing you do, plays mind games with you as if you are totally incompetent; shoots down any new ideas you bring to the table, and has no intention of changing his or her mind because he or she is stuck in their ways. This can be a very frustrating situation. Suddenly, you find out that your boss is leaving and a new manager is coming in. When the new manager comes, he or she asks that you provide them with input on all major decisions. Instead of taking the bull by the horns, you state that you are not ready for the daunting tasks and you are afraid of making a major mistake. You have a great *opportunity*, but due to the low expectations your previous boss placed on you, your confidence was diminished to a point that you called this *grand opportunity* an *insurmountable obstacle*.

This is what happened to the Children of Israel when they spied out the land of Canaan, the Promised Land. God Almighty had *already* promised the land to them, but when they spied it out, they noticed that a *host* of obstacles stood in the way of seeing the Promised Land clearly. There were *giants* in the land, *warriors* in the land, and several nations that were enemies of God, all in the land that had their names on it! How did the majority of the spies react to this spiritual irritation? Like any of us would today. They stated that although the land had a wealth of opportunity, harvest, resources, and prosperity, there were too many *obstacles* in the way. The spies felt outnumbered, out-gunned (sword), and out-smarted by so vast of an opposition. However, there were *two* spies that saw the *same* obstacles, but from a *different vantage* point. The spies' names were Joshua and Caleb. They didn't *ignore* the hindrances of the giants and warriors in the land, they just didn't give these giants "all" power status in their lives. They knew they would have to fight, but the victory *belonged* to God. You see, Joshua and Caleb knew God for who He is, the All-powerful One. They knew that God had given the children of Israel a promise. They knew that God had their back, front, side, bottom and top. They understood how God operated because they had a deep *personal relationship* with the Almighty Creator of the universe. They knew that *God was Almighty! Do you still believe that He is almighty in your personal life today?*

God never loses a battle. He never gets tired. He always keeps His Word and promises. Joshua and Caleb had this information and were *persuaded* that they could take the land today! Joshua *saw* the power of God, first hand. He was Moses' assistant. He was close to Moses when Moses spoke to God, face-to-face. He was in Moses' *inner circle* of friends. Let me ask you a question: *Who's in your inner circle? Who's inner circle are you in?* Moses trained Joshua in all facets of the ministry and mentored him well. You see how your *vocabulary* changes based on those you fellowship with? As I stated before and will continue to state throughout this book, if you hang around fools, you will start *thinking, talking,* and *acting* like them. If you hang around a*dulterers*, you will formulate a flirtatious and promiscuous spirit. If you hang around *crooks*, you will develop a *criminal* mind-set.

However, if you hang around the *wise*, you will increase in wisdom. If you hang around *faithful* & *trustworthy* people, you will develop a deeper faithfulness. If you hang around an *entrepreneur*, you may develop a CEO mindset. Why do you think college students intern at companies during their junior or senior years, unpaid? I'll tell you why. As students matriculate towards graduation, they *know* that their mindset must match the next level of their career. It would not be profitable for a student to finish college, only to be fired from his or her first job. There are unwritten rules that these students need to discover so they can be competitive, are promoted and contribute the mission of their future employer. Therefore, colleges *force* their students to grow intellectually by *requiring* juniors and seniors to intern in order to earn their degree. As a result, the graduate will be able to land employment and handle the new challenges they might face in this new chapter of their career. If you hang around *leaders*, you may refine your leadership skills. Joshua hung around Moses, and Caleb hung around Joshua and the rest is history. Caleb knew what Joshua knew and accepted God's Word and Laws as *final*. Moreover, both were richly blessed on *Earth* for their faith!

I want to extract a very important point here about God. He *may not* always remove the *obstacles*. Nevertheless, you have to believe Him and walk in your belief to watch Him deliver every time. You might be in the midst of applying for a promotion or powerful job (promise land) that you are *qualified* to secure. You may not *look* like the people in the offices higher up. You may not be the *gender* of those applying for the position. You may not have the same *traditional educational pedigree* of those who are applying for the position. You may not be a part of the same *traditional political* or *fraternal affiliation* of those vying for the same position. You may not be the *traditional race* or *ethnicity* of those jockeying for the position, but you and God know that He has already promised you the position. This is where faith shines the brightest.

You have a cataclysmic decision to make. You can respond like the 10 spies who acknowledged the opportunity, but *amplified* the obstacles; or you could walk in the spirit of Caleb and Joshua who *focused on God's strong arm* of *victory* and deliverance. For example, you may have struggled through several years of college, working your fingers to the bone in an effort to maintain a strong GPA, stay on schedule, and market yourself as a competitive selection for a career in your field of study. You graduate, only to find that there are more applicants than jobs. What do you do? Your competition may have graduated with a higher GPA; come from an Ivy-League school; or may have fraternity brothers or sorority sisters in the position to hire them on the spot. However, let me tell you something that carries much weight. If you *know* God and have surrendered to Him by *living* by His Word and *trusting* in His name, don't let the *giants* (competition) stop you from *applying* for that job, *picking up* the phone, or *submitting* your resume online! You are *more* than able to get that position today! It's just an *opportunity* for God to show up and move in a mighty way on your behalf. My friend, God is the great Equalizer!

Although the children of Israel followed the majority vote (limitation), God still honored both Joshua and Caleb for trusting His word. For example, Joshua succeeded Moses as the leader of the children of Israel and Caleb lived through the

Wilderness experience. The entire generation over 20 years of age died in the wilderness, except Joshua and Caleb. Both Joshua and Caleb walked into the Promise land and experienced the flowing milk and honey of blessings associated with Canaan. This is what I like about God here. No matter what family you come from, if you make up your mind that you will *serve* the Lord and honor Him in your lifestyle, actions, beliefs, and speech, God can elevate you above the trap of low expectations and generational curses. It simply rests with you deciding that you will serve the Lord.

Discussion Questions

1. How did Joshua and Caleb view the obstacles of the Promised Land?

2. Why is it important to follow God's voice? What are the consequences of not trusting God in your life?

3. Read **James 1: 5-7**. What does God promise to those who ask for wisdom?

4. Read **Jeremiah 29:11**. What does God intend for those who follow Him wholeheartedly?

5. Read **Jeremiah 9:23-24**. What is God impressed with?

PART IV

ENCOURAGE YOURSELF: TAPPING INTO YOUR POWER SOURCE

Pillar 12: Brand Yourself: What's Your Imprint?

"Everybody has a fan."--Dr. Lamont Ricks

When you hear the following names, *McDonald's, Burger King, Chick-fil-A, Pizza Hut, and Golden Corral* what comes to mind? Well, food surely comes to mind, but each of the aforementioned names have specialties that distinguish their business from their competitors. Chick-fil-A is known for its *juicy chicken sandwiches*. McDonald's is known for its *fries*. Burger King is known for its *Whopper Burger*, and Golden Corral is known for its *buffet*. Do you know that God created you to be *known* for something? Maybe, it's your voice, your artistic ability, your mechanical skill, your leadership qualities, or your orator skills. You were created to do *something* great for His Glory and your edification. This is why it is of prime importance that you develop a *personal brand.* A *personal brand* is an individual's set of chief attributes that they are defined by. When it comes to Biblical characters, we may have our favorites. For example, *Job* of Uz was known for his *patience* under *physical and emotional distress. King David* was known for his *courage, leadership,* and *valiant* spirit in battle. *Gideon,* an Israeli judge/general, was known for his 300 men of valor who dismantled, *with* God's help, over 180,000 enemy soldiers. *Moses* and *Joshua* were both known for their highly coveted *leadership skills* and *strategic thinking skills. Samson,* an Israeli judge, was known for his *super-human strength. Daniel,* the Hebrew exile of Babylon, was known for his *consistent prayer life, administrative acumen, boldness* and *understanding. King Solomon* was known for his *extraordinary wisdom* and wealth. The prostitute *Rehab,* who we will discuss in detail later, was known for her *bravery* and *faith* in God's messengers. The three Hebrew slaves, *Shadrach, Meshach,* and *Abednego,* were all known for their *one-ness* of mind, *strong faith,* and *unwavering courage* when facing a horrible death at the hands King Nebedcunezzer (Daniel 3). There are many other figures in the Bible who *branded* themselves for God's glory, resulting in millions of believers *throughout* history. Now, what do all of these characters have in common? They all placed their total faith and trust in the mighty hand of God. Whatever they did, they performed the task *consistently.* Consistency is the *precursor* to branding.

Dr. Ricks Branding Model (2012)

CONSISTENCY + ENVIRONMENT+OPPORTUNITY+ BEHAVIOR+ ENVIRONMENTAL RESPONSE=BRANDING

(C+E+O+B+ER=BRND)

In my branding model, *consistency* means having a non-stop drive, focus, and state of mind to accomplish a task for a greater purpose, no matter what comes your way. The *Environment* is the setting or place one finds himself/herself affixed, or in some cases trapped. This could be as small as a community neighborhood, or as large as an entire culture. *Opportunities* are situations that occur to the person being tested. Opportunities can be both *positive* and *negative*. However, the tested individual somehow finds a way to use the opportunity to his or her *advantage. Behaviors* are the actions and beliefs one executes in order to accomplish a settled purpose. *Environmental Responses* are the reactions or agreements of the people who are impacted and influenced by the person's behavior.

Let me ask some *very serious* questions. *What are you known for? Are you known for your work ethic? Are you known for your intelligence? What about the way you carry yourself in public? Do people gravitate towards you when you speak? When you walk into a room, does it light up? Are you known for your professionalism on the job? What do people say about you, particularly those in your inner circle?*

On the contrary, *are you known for flirtatious speech? Are you known for telling dirty, X-rated jokes? Are you known for blowing up on people for the smallest infraction? Are you known for being the office gossip? Are you known for slandering the boss' name in the mud? Are you known to break your promises to your children? Are you known to disrespect your spouse in public? Are you known to disrespect authority figures? Are you known for cursing at your parents, teachers, or administrators? Are you known for skipping school? Are you known to involve yourself in risky sexual activity?* Ask yourself, what are you known for? It might surprise you. The aforementioned questions are not an exhaustive list, but it is a great start to self-evaluation. *Branding* is not based on *who* you say you are, but the daily actions you exhibit before friends, relatives, co-workers, *and* your critics. I am fully aware that no one is perfect, but we should all strive to become better each day. If *what* you say you are *does not* line up with your *daily actions*, then you need to ask God for forgiveness. Asking for forgiveness is no walk in the park. It takes a load of humility, which we as humans are not wired to exhibit. But let me tell you, there is no better feeling than to know a huge burden has been lifted off of your shoulders when you make the *attempt* to be forgiven. Remember, God, Who is good all of the time, died on the cross so that we could be forgiven, cleansed, and justified from all of our sins for all time (1 Peter 3:18).

Pillar 13: The Power of Prayer

"4When he had seized him, he put him in prison, delivering him to four squads of soldiers to guard him, intending after the Passover to bring him out before the people. 5So Peter was kept in the prison, but prayer for him was being made fervently by the church to God. 6On the very night when Herod was about to bring him forward, Peter was sleeping between two soldiers, bound with two chains, and guards in front of the door were watching over the prison. 7And behold, an angel of the Lord suddenly appeared and a light shone in the cell; and he struck Peter's side and woke him up, saying, "Get up quickly " And his chains fell off his hands."--
Acts 12:4-6 (NASB)

Can you imagine being thrown into a prison for preaching your Faith? Can you think how you would feel knowing that the person in charge of the Law hated you based solely upon your Faith? This was the situation the Apostle Peter found himself in. All of the odds were stacked against him. Death was not only probable, but certain. James, the brother of John, one of Jesus' disciples, had been executed before Peter went to prison for sharing the Gospel of Jesus Christ. Wow, what persecution the early church leaders faced on a daily basis. We should be counting our blessings for living in America where we can appreciate a multitude of freedoms, particularly religious ones! We should not take this for granted.

King Herod, ruler of a roman province, was a very powerful, violent, and cruel individual. He killed Christians for sport, was known to execute criminals in a savage manner, and had a god complex. In 2013, I still hear a lot of people use the title *god* to describe themselves. They walk around stating that they are little gods. Until you can live *without* food, shelter, water and oxygen, walk through solid walls, manipulate time, control Hurricanes and Tsunamis, you cannot form your *lips* to say that you are a god. Really?! A god of what: foolishness? Everything humanity has, uses, and even pursues in this life was made available because the *Living God* allowed it to be. My friend, please *don't* fall into the trap of calling yourself a god. This is *not* a good form of *self-esteem building*. It will just build a case against you for the Living God to destroy. Don't test Him. When you can die and raise yourself from the dead, walk on water, or turn water into wine, then I would say you have an argument to call yourself a god; but we all know that you can't stop a speeding bullet or out run a freight train, so I can't even call you *superman*! Moreover, superman didn't even say he was a god.

King Herod was also instrumental in the crucifixion of Jesus Christ on the cross, (a very popular) Roman method of execution. Imagine what was going through Peter's mind. The Jewish people who opposed Christ and everything Christian were pleased that Herod had executed James, now it was Peter's turn to feel the wrath of his cold steel. Herod's mind was made up. What a way to gain the attention of the Jewish people under Roman rule. What epic moment this must have been for Herod to do what no other Roman Ruler had ever conceived, kill the

Lamb of God (Jesus) *and* the leader of the Disciples?! That would definitely propel him to become the next Emperor. However, God blocked his wicked scheme to kill Peter. You see, the text clearly states that a *group* of believers, who took their relationship with God seriously, were away at a house praying for Peter's escape. We are not talking about "cliché-rich" praying, where you say, *"Lord, let thy will be done...whatever happens, happens."*

I want to make a point very clear here my friend. We serve a God of detail *and* specifics. I've always said and will *continue* to assert that I *do not* want you praying *generalized* prayers over me. Be specific! Suppose you were diagnosed with Lung Cancer. You don't want the preacher praying... *"Lord, whatever you decide, you'll do...Amen."* No, no, no! Honestly, I may get upset and say some unkind words and tell him to leave my bed side, with a little attitude in my weakened voice. This is a *critical* time in my life. Time is of essence here. I want the seasoned and devout prayer warriors, who have tested God through *earnest prayer*, on my behalf to inundate me with prayer. I want a *strong* Christian man or woman to lay hands on my lung area, anoint me with oil, and pray something like(just an example):

> *"Lord Jesus, You are the creator and architect of the body. You know exactly what needs to be done to restore my dear brother to health. You can easily speak to the cancer in his Lung and it must obey Your command like when you spoke to the Red Sea, like you spoke to the Lions in the den, like you spoke to the fish that swallowed Jonah, like*

you spoke to Death to release Lazarus, like you spoke to the Jordan River, and like you spoke to the earth to tremble. I know and believe, with full confidence in your power, that you are able to wipe this cancer out of his body miraculously. If it be your will, Father, please hear our cry for restoration of health that you will get the glory! Amen."

You see the vast difference here? Now, I know some of you who are reading this book are from the *super-spiritual* group who says, God is Omniscient (All-knowing) so we don't need to get all *wordy* with our requests. He knows our thoughts before we ask of Him. Yes, my brother or sister, *you are correct.* He does know every thought; but you are focused on the *wrong* point of prayer. It's not about being *wordy* or *articulate,* it's about being *detailed* and *specific.* There is a *distinction.* For example, if you are a <u>married</u> man, I promise you that your wife will ask you the million dollar question, *"Honey, how do I look?"* Men, this is a *general* question, but it *demands* the most detailed answer(s) from you. When this question is posed, you can interpret it in a myriad of ways, but you better get it right or you are toast. A woman desires to be reassured and validated by her man that she looks *stunning.* So simply saying, *"Honey, you look nice"* won't get you any *cool points* with your woman. And don't expect any loving that night, you can forget it. What your spouse is *really* asking includes, but not limited to the following: *How does my hair look? How does my physical body look? Do I look unattractive? Do my wrinkles show? How does my skin look with and without make-up? Am I appealing to you after all these years together? How do these earrings bring out my eye color? Do you like my French manicure, etc..?* I know I just helped some *married* men out with that list. You will be surprised how far you will get when you answer your wife in *positive, reassuring, self-esteem building* detail. The whole point I want to drive home here is that God created us with *detail* in mind.

We serve a God of *detail.* How do I know that to be true? Well, just look all around at Nature. Look at how beautiful and *detailed* the flowers in your garden are; the colors, the fragrances, the inner-workings of each pedal. Look at the bugs and birds. They are so diverse; each species has intricate *detail.* God's workmanship is all around us. We are immersed in His *"detail."* However, mankind are the only created beings who *refuse* to give God what He desires most; that is, our worship of Him in *detail.*

Now let's get back to Peter. He was shackled between two Roman soldiers and two more soldiers were positioned at the door to ensure that Peter couldn't escape. Now, four squadrons mean that there was a rotation of four fresh soldiers to guard Peter from thinking about leaving. The Romans were experts at building prisons and executing people. A Roman soldier committed his very life to Rome. He was not allowed to marry. He was trained to march 20 miles without resources, and able to kill on site with a ferocious skill. He would give the Navy Seals of today a run for their money. Peter was doomed! But wait: verse 5 injects hope into the situation. The Bible declares, *"that while he was in prison, people of the church of God prayed without ceasing for Peter."* Now let's look at some key words. The Bible says that they prayed for him "without ceasing (non-stop or continual)". Here you have a group of devout Christian brothers and sisters who are petitioning the Almighty God for Peter's protection, release, and God's divine intervention. The Bible says that while Peter was sleeping between two Roman soldiers, bound with two chains, an Angel of God came to him. A light shone in the prison; the angel smote Peter on the side and said, "Get up quickly". The chains fell off Peter. The Angel went on to tell Peter to *"gird himself". That is, get your wits about you, wake up and follow me.* The verses go on to state that when they reached an outer gate it opened by itself (without human assistance). What a miracle! Prayer ushers in miracles into our lives. You see, my friend, serious prayer can go places we cannot physically go. Prayer can reach people who are far away. You don't have to live in the same state or even country of an individual to effectively pray for them to be delivered. I would like to compare prayer to carbon monoxide (CO). Carbon monoxide is a very dangerous gas. If you own a home, you are encouraged by the Fire department to invest in a $20.00 CO detector. You see, scientifically speaking, CO is not detected by any of the human senses. You cannot smell, taste, see, touch, or hear CO. This is why it is so dangerous. It will kill you if you inhale too much of it. Anatomically, CO pulls the iron ions out of human blood and does not release these ions. Now, Dr. Ricks, what does that have to do with anything? It has a lot to do with it. The iron ions in our blood carries O_2 (oxygen) to our lungs, heart, and brain. No oxygen equals suffocation, which equals certain death. Do you get my point? Prayer is like *spiritual* carbon monoxide to the kingdom of darkness. When we pray for our loved-ones and friends who may be shackled by drug addiction, sexual addiction, anger addiction, a lying or cheating spirit, or occult brainwashing, it can cause the demonic strongholds to suffocate, thus releasing our love ones from the grip of addiction and the slavery to their sin. When we understand the potency of serious prayer, we will free many people from all types of bondage. So the next time you get on your knees or are driving in your car, realize how powerful *prayer* is. It can break the yoke of bondage off you and the ones you love! The book of **James, chapter 5:13-19** triumphantly states:

> " 13 *Is anyone among you suffering? Then he must pray. Is anyone cheerful? He is to sing praises.* 14 *Is anyone among you sick? Then he must call for the elders of the church and they are to pray over him, anointing him with oil in the name of the Lord;* 15 *and the prayer offered in faith will restore the one who is sick, and the Lord will raise him up, and if he has committed sins, they will be forgiven him.* 16 *Therefore, confess your sins to one another, and pray for one another so that you may be healed. The effective prayer of a righteous man can accomplish much.* 17 *Elijah was a man with a nature like ours, and he prayed earnestly that it would not rain, and it did not rain on the*

earth for three years and six months. ¹⁸ *Then he prayed again, and the sky poured rain and the earth produced its fruit."* (NASB)

Do you ever find yourself getting distracted when you want to pray? How about this one, do your ever get very sleepy at night when you desire to pray or read your Bible? I know I do. But can I get real with you? No Christian is immune to sin's mighty grip, no one! All of us have certain sins that can get our undivided attention at weird hours of the night. I've heard of some Christians, who struggle with drinking, getting up out of bed at 2 AM to drive to a store to buy an alcoholic beverage to satisfy their taste. Others, who may struggle with drugs, are said to have driven all over town in their pajamas to find a narcotics dealer. I've even heard of some Christians, who struggle with sexual addiction, staying up to 4 AM viewing pornographic images and using their credit cards to pay for adult films via the internet, knowing that they have to get up at 7AM to report to their jobs. The point I want to stress here is that sin is very *powerful, seductive, secretive*, and *satisfying* for a *season*. However, the *consequences* of our sins are immeasurable. Sin's seduction is nothing to be trifled with. It is *not* worth it. Sin's cravings can cause *all* of us to do things that we should *not* do.

I would like to submit that when you are trying to read the Bible and *suddenly* get sleepy, it is not *always* physiological, but *sometimes* spiritual. We are in an intense spiritual warfare with the kingdom of darkness, our own flesh nature, and the world's system of beliefs. The Christian is under constant attack on the battleground of the mind. Have you ever been praying and a negative thought crossed your mind? That's not a coincidence. That was a spiritual attack. Look at **James 5:13-19** again. Prayer can heal and usher miracles into our lives. Satan does not want the power of God to move in your life, so he blocks our prayers to the Almighty God *via* temptation and diversions of the mind. If Satan can *weaken* our communication with God (prayer), he can creep into our lives and destroy us, limb from limb. My friend, when you go to bed, remember to pray for someone who may be *chained* down by sin. The deliverance may *only* come through *your* efforts. Fight hard!

Pillar 14: Power of Unbelief

"²⁴Then the LORD rained on Sodom and Gomorrah brimstone and fire from the LORD out of heaven,²⁵and He overthrew those cities, and all the valley, and all the inhabitants of the cities, and what grew on the ground.²⁶But his wife, from behind him, looked back, and she became a pillar of salt."- -Genesis 19:24-26 (NASB)

Earth, wind, and fire are described as some of the most fearsome forces of Nature; but in the spiritual and emotional realm, "unbelief" is far worse than Hurricane Katrina, the Chilean Earthquake, and the Japanese Tsunami put together. Why is unbelief so critical to the human experience? Well, all supernatural and miraculous acts are exclusively based on the premise of *believing* in God's mighty hand to work out our problems. In **Hebrews 11:1** and **6**, it reads:

> *"Now faith is the assurance of things hoped for, the conviction of things not seen. ² For by it the men of old gained approval.³ By faith we understand that the worlds were prepared by the word of God, so that what is seen was not made out of things which are visible. ⁴ By faith Abel offered to God a better sacrifice than Cain, through which he obtained the testimony that he was righteous, God testifying about his gifts, and through faith, though he is dead, he still speaks. ⁵ By faith Enoch was taken up so that he would not see death; AND HE WAS NOT FOUND BECAUSE GOD TOOK HIM UP; for he obtained the witness that before his being taken up he was pleasing to God. ⁶ And without faith it is impossible to please Him, for he who comes to God must believe that He is and that He is a rewarder of those who seek Him. ⁷ By faith Noah, being*

warned by God about things not yet seen, in reverence prepared an ark for the salvation of his household, by which he condemned the world, and became an heir of the righteousness which is according to faith." (NASB)

Before we can *truly* understand what *unbelief* is, we need to dig into the seriousness of *belief.* For the sake of argument, I will use the word *Faith* instead. What is faith? Well, there are *several* definitions that man has conjured up to describe faith, but I want to see *God's* definition of faith. The Bible will tell us this definition. The book of Hebrews, chapter 11 verse one says, "Now Faith is the substance of things hoped for and the evidence (conviction) of things not seen (with the *naked eye*)". So, we see faith is the *substance* of whatever you desire to happen in your life. It is the evidence (before it occurs) of that thing that has not happened yet. In other words, it is an unwavering determination that you cannot shake. What a beautiful *phenomenon. Faith* is the *engine of hope*; that is, it *fuels* hope. *Hopelessness* is an *underrated* variable in the human experience. When *hopelessness* kicks in, you are in *grave* danger. Many terminally ill people have given up the fight for their health because *hopelessness* overcame them. Many criminals will go on a killing spree and interrupt the normalcy of everyday life because they have gone beyond the point of no return and have lost all *hope.* A percentage of women will turn to *lesbianism* because they have lost *hope* of finding a loving man. Some men and women will enter into a promiscuous lifestyle because they have given up on the tradition of celibacy until marriage. Young boys will continue to join *gangs* and get involved in juvenile delinquency because the *absence* of the father figure, which has produced generational *hopelessness*. Some people will turn to alcohol and drugs, which is a doorway to a plethora of personal problems because of *hopelessness*. Marriages and other relationships drown in the sea of pressure and frustration because of *hopelessness*. You see, if I can make you "feel" that you have no hope in a given situation, you *will* give up and eventually empty yourself of responsibility, accountability, and opportunity to turn your life around. I have talked to many people who have allowed hopelessness to overwhelm them and become a *dominant* force in their lives. I've spoken to individuals with long criminal pasts who express self-defeating thoughts about starting a successful career. I have seen others *give up* on losing weight because no matter how much they count calories, walk on the treadmill, and cut out sweets, the scale doesn't change by much. *Hope* is like the wheels of a truck. I don't care how beautiful the exterior or how plush the interior, if a vehicle does not have any wheels it will not move an inch! Are you walking with me? If a person in your life or a situation causes you to lose *hope* in God and in self, you will remain a shell of what God has created you to be. No matter what condition you may find yourself in, *faith* can cause the invisible to pierce the visible world. However, you must have a "do or die" approach to faith for it to work for you. We must remember that faith is always married to *works*, not merely *words*. Many people offer a lot of lip service; they "talk" a good game, but their feet stay planted in the soil of *unbelief.*

On November 9, 1996 my all-time favorite boxer, Evander "The Real Deal" Holyfield, took on the monumental challenge of fighting "Iron Mike Tyson," the most feared and respected boxer since Ali, George Forman, and Joe Frazier. During the press conferences, Holyfield never backed down from the heavier, stockier, intimidating and more powerful Tyson. Tyson's notorious and infamous stare downs did not shake or faze Holyfield. When asked who would win the bout, Holyfield *prophetically* stated that with God's help, he would be victorious. The sports commentators dismissed Holyfield's religious statements as superstitious rhetoric. The critics had Tyson winning by a Technical Knockout (TKO), but as the sports records indicate, Evander beat Tyson *two* times: first in 1996 and second in 1997 (although, enduring an "ear biting" injury). Evander is the only 5-time Heavyweight champion. The great Muhammad Ali cannot even <u>boast</u> that.

Are you in the fight of your life? Is your marriage on the rocks? Are your children defying your authority to no end? Is your home up for foreclosure? Are you behind on your school loans? Is your job being threatened by downsizing? Is that former drug or sexual addiction calling your name? Did the cancer come back a *third* time? Is your spouse threatening a divorce? What is it that has opposed you and is trying to TKO your life's purpose?

The Bible is full of examples of people who *walked out* their faith and overcame bad situations in their lives. Let me call to the scene, David, the shepherd boy and anointed King of Israel. Read **1 Samuel 17: 1-4; 8-11; 26-37**

> "*1 Now the Philistines gathered their armies for battle; and they were gathered at Socoh which belongs to Judah, and they camped between Socoh and Azekah, in Ephes-dammim. 2 Saul and the men of Israel were gathered and camped in the valley of Elah, and drew up in battle array to encounter the Philistines. 3 The Philistines stood on the mountain on one side while Israel stood on the mountain on the other side, with the valley between them. 4 Then a champion came out from the armies of the Philistines named Goliath, from Gath, whose height was six cubits and a span .8 He stood and shouted to the ranks of Israel and said to them, "Why do you come out to draw up in battle array? Am I not the Philistine and you servants of Saul? Choose a man for yourselves and let him come down to me. 9 If he is able to fight with me and kill me, then we will become your servants; but if I prevail against him and kill him, then you shall become our servants and serve us." 10 Again the Philistine said, "I defy the ranks of Israel this day; give me a man that we may fight together." 11 When Saul and all Israel heard these words of the Philistine, they were dismayed and greatly afraid. 26 Then David spoke to the men who were standing by him, saying, "What will be done for the man who kills this Philistine and takes away the reproach from Israel? For who is this uncircumcised Philistine, that he should taunt the armies of the living God?" 27 The people answered him in accord with this*

word, saying, "Thus it will be done for the man who kills him." *28 Now Eliab his oldest brother heard when he spoke to the men; and Eliab's anger burned against David and he said, "Why have you come down? And with whom have you left those few sheep in the wilderness? I know your insolence and the wickedness of your heart; for you have come down in order to see the battle." 29 But David said, "What have I done now? Was it not just a question?" 30 Then he turned away from him to another and said the same thing; and the people answered the same thing as before." (NASB)*

David Wins Against All Odds

"31 When the words which David spoke were heard, they told them to Saul, and he sent for him. 32 David said to Saul, "Let no man's heart fail on account of him; your servant will go and fight with this Philistine." 33 Then Saul said to David, "You are not able to go against this Philistine to fight with him; for you are but a youth while he has been a warrior from his youth." 34 But David said to Saul, "Your servant was tending his father's sheep. When a lion or a bear came and took a lamb from the flock, 35 I went out after him and attacked him, and rescued it from his mouth; and when he rose up against me, I seized him by his beard and struck him and killed him. 36 Your servant has killed both the lion and the bear; and this uncircumcised Philistine will be like one of them, since he has taunted the armies of the living God." 37 And David said, "The LORD who delivered me from the paw of the lion and from the paw of the bear, He will deliver me from the hand of this Philistine." And Saul said to David, "Go, and may the LORD be with you." (NASB)

What a tremendous story of real, biblical faith! This story is pregnant with promises and provisions that God affords to His children; only if they take Him at His word and walk out their faith in Him. Here we have the youngest of eight boys. The *unlikely,* hero of the day, David did not allow the insults of his flesh and blood (Eliab) to sway his destiny of becoming great. You see, whether you know it or not, you have a *seed* of greatness in you. However, it is up to you to develop, water, and cultivate the blessed seed of greatness. God will not do this for you, it's up to you.

Take Back Your Blessings

There is so much that can be gleaned from this heroic story of David against Goliath, but I want to focus on something that is rarely talked about when we look at David. You rarely hear discussion about the "lion and the bear." That's right, the lion and the bear. David's confidence and security came from the victories of his past. Think for a minute of the victories of your past. Can you identify some situations, persons, or mind-sets that you had to overcome in order to get where you are today? Maybe you had a deadly illness God healed you from, or an abusive and/or cheating partner that God delivered you from. Maybe God delivered you through difficult coursework in college in order for you to graduate. I don't know what it could have been, but I know this; God stepped in at the perfect time and gave you power to overcome your adversity. This is what David knew. Let's look at the significance of David's statement. One, electricity was not in existence during the time David had to fight the lion and the bear. Animals can see in the dark, humans cannot. Two, both the Lion and bear are carnivorous, strong, ferocious animals that could kill a man in seconds with a swipe of their paws. Third, the Bible states the sheep were already inside of the mouths of the lion and bear. Now, anyone with half a brain knows that once a lion or bear gets a defenseless animal in its crushing jaws, the animal is as *good as dead*. But not David! His faith in God was so strong that no matter what the odds, visible circumstances, or creatures were doing with their teeth, he continued to go after his sheep. Think about it; he left all of the other 'un-tainted" sheep and ran after a 300 pound lion and a 500-800+ pound bear! Wow! That is faith out of this world! You see, David's relationship to God and his commitment to his sheep outweighed his concern for his physical well-being. Do you know that God has given you many blessings in this life to own and use, but some of your blessing are caught in the mouths of lions and bears of this world? It is entirely up to you (with God's help) to go after them and take your blessings back, but you are going to have to "fight" with every strained of effort to do so. What do you believe about your future? Do you believe that your dreams can be realized? Do you believe that you can overcome fear? Do you believe that your current situation can change for the better, financially, socially, or emotionally? Well, you have to believe *beyond* your human efforts. That is, you have to have FAITH in God's mighty hand to move you from *this* place in life to the *next* level in life. It can be accomplished. One of the biggest lies that many people, Christians and non-believers alike, succumb to is that *all* of your blessings are within arms' reach. This is totally <u>FALSE</u>. The three Hebrew boys had to go through a "fiery furnace" before they earned respect from King Nebednezzur. Daniel had to be thrown into a lion's den before he silenced his *haters* and was promoted by King Darius. Joseph was beaten by his blood brothers, sold into slavery, lied on by Potiphar's wife, and spent over 13 years in prison for a crime he did not commit before he became ruler of Egypt! What is my point in telling you all of this? Well, some of God's blessings that have your name on it were "created" inside of the lion's mouth of life. With God's help and acting out your faith in Him, He will give you the courage, commitment, and tenacity to crush your opposition and tear down the walls that erect themselves in your life. Power Up!

Pillar 15: Decisions Equate to Destination

"How do you overcome stupidity? Make one good decision after another."—Dr. Lamont Ricks

Decisions, decisions, decisions... Did you know that you are the sum total of the daily decisions you make? This chapter focuses on such an important topic. All of us can look back across the precipice of our lives with a 20/20 vision and say, *"Wow, I should've done it that way instead of this way."* Don't worry; several successful individuals have made a ton of poor choices in their past, but there is a blessing: no matter what season or quarter you find yourself in life, you *can* change the game before you close your eyes one last time in the land of the living. You know, so many people fall into a deep depression or despair because they have "allowed" the devil to replay past poor decisions in their minds over and over and over. Like a video set on a repeating loop, Satan whispers in our minds,

> *"You are such a screw-up." "You are a fool." "What an idiot." "You don't deserve to live." "You are no good, just scum at the bottom of a toilet." "You will always be a....."* *"No one could ever marry someone who did what you did..." "If your parents only knew how much alcohol ingested or dope you smoked..." "If your pastor knew how filthy you were in the past, He wouldn't let you minister to anyone in the church"*

On and on like a broken turntable, these self-defeating thoughts swim through our minds. You feel as though you have no value to help someone else in his or her trials because of the sinful things you did in your past, but this is all a Big LIE. You see, I want you to know a powerful truth. No matter what you've done in your past; *adultery, drugs, fraud, armed robbery, murder, prostitution, lying, cheating, or stealing*, God came to Earth to pay for *all* of your sins on the cross. Let's look at one individual who made many bad decisions in her life, but with God's help and intervention, she turned her destructive lifestyle into a notable life of *faith* and *honor*.

Rahab (The Prostitute of Jericho)

The book of Joshua chapter 2 introduces us to a prostitute named Rahab. Her vocation was having sex for money. I'm sure some of her clients included soldiers of Jericho and wayward husbands. She probably destroyed many marriages and led weak men astray because of their sexual practices. On one particular day, something dramatic happened when Joshua sent spies out to Jericho to engage in battle. This long acting prostitute made a change. She did something that was out of the ordinary. She hid the spies of Israel in her house from Jericho's King and armed men. Please read the following passage and observe how this *woman of the night* became a woman of God, due to *one* very pivotal decision. One *decision* changed this woman's eternal destination and legacy.

" Then Joshua the son of Nun sent two men as spies secretly from Shittim, saying, "Go, and view the land, especially Jericho." So they went and came into the house of a harlot whose name was Rahab, and lodged there. 2 It was told the king of Jericho, saying, "Behold, men from the sons of Israel have come here tonight to search out the land." 3 And the king of Jericho sent word to Rahab, saying, "Bring out the men who have come to you, who have entered your house, for they have come to search out all the land." 4 But the woman had taken the two men and hidden them, and she said, "Yes, the men came to me, but I did not know where they were from. 5 It came about when it was time to shut the gate at dark that the men went out; I do not know where the men went. Pursue them quickly, for you will overtake them." 6 But she had brought them up to the roof and hidden them in the stalks of flax which she had laid in order on the roof. 7 So the men pursued them on the road to the Jordan to the fords; and as soon as those who were pursuing them had gone out, they shut the gate. 8 Now before they lay down, she came up to them on the roof, 9 and said to the men, "I know that the LORD has given you the land, and that the terror of you has fallen on us, and that all the inhabitants of the land have melted away before you. 10 For we have heard how the LORD dried up the water of the Red Sea before you when you came out of Egypt, and what you did to the two kings of the Amorites who were beyond the Jordan, to Sihon and Og, whom you utterly destroyed. 11 When we heard it, our hearts melted and no courage remained in any man any longer because of you; for the LORD your God, He is God in heaven above and on earth beneath. 12 Now therefore, please swear to me by the LORD, since I have dealt kindly with you, that you also will deal kindly with my father's household, and give me a pledge of truth, 13 and spare my father and my mother and my brothers and my sisters, with all who belong to them, and deliver our lives from death." 14 So the men said to her, "Our life for yours if you do not tell this business of ours; and it

shall come about when the LORD *gives us the land that we will deal kindly and ⁽ⁱ⁾faithfully with you."* (NASB)

The Promise to Rahab

"15 Then she let them down by a rope through the window, for her house was on the city wall, so that she was living on the wall. 16 She said to them, "Go to the hill country, so that the pursuers will not happen upon you, and hide yourselves there for three days until the pursuers return. Then afterward you may go on your way." 17 The men said to her, "We shall be free from this oath to you which you have made us swear, 18 unless, when we come into the land, you tie this cord of scarlet thread in the window through which you let us down, and gather to yourself into the house your father and your mother and your brothers and all your father's household. 19 It shall come about that anyone who goes out of the doors of your house into the street, his blood shall be on his own head, and we shall be free; but anyone who is with you in the house, his blood shall be on our head if a hand is laid on him. 20 But if you tell this business of ours, then we shall be free from the oath which you have made us swear." 21 She said, "According to your words, so be it." So she sent them away, and they departed; and she tied the scarlet cord in the window.22 They departed and came to the hill country, and remained there for three days until the pursuers returned. Now the pursuers had sought them all along the road, but had not found them. 23 Then the two men returned and came down from the hill country and crossed over and came to Joshua the son of Nun, and they related to him all that had happened to them. 24 They said to Joshua, "Surely the LORD *has given all the land into our hands; moreover, all the inhabitants of the land have melted away before us."* (NASB)

The Reward for Rahab's Fear of The Lord God

*"7 The city and all that is in it are to be devoted to the
LORD. Only Rahab the prostitute and all who are with her
in her house shall be spared, because she hid the spies we
sent. 18 But keep away from the devoted things, so that you
will not bring about your own destruction by taking any
of them. Otherwise you will make the camp of Israel liable
to destruction and bring trouble on it. 19 All the silver and
gold and the articles of bronze and iron are sacred to the
LORD and must go into his treasury."20 When the trumpets
sounded, the army shouted, and at the sound of the
trumpet, when the men gave a loud shout, the wall
collapsed; so everyone charged straight in, and they took
the city. 21 They devoted the city to the LORD and destroyed
with the sword every living thing in it—men and women,
young and old, cattle, sheep and donkeys.22 Joshua said to
the two men who had spied out the land, "Go into the
prostitute's house and bring her out and all who belong to
her, in accordance with your oath to her." 23 So the young
men who had done the spying went in and brought out
Rahab, her father and mother, her brothers and sisters
and all who belonged to her. They brought out her entire
family and put them in a place outside the camp of
Israel.24 Then they burned the whole city and everything in
it, but they put the silver and gold and the articles of
bronze and iron into the treasury of the LORD's house.
25 But Joshua spared Rahab the prostitute, with her family
and all who belonged to her, because she hid the men
Joshua had sent as spies to Jericho—and she lives among
the Israelites to this day." (NASB)*

Wow! What an amazing account of *real* faith. Real faith will

cost you something. Rahab could have snitched on these foreign

spies and foiled Joshua's plans. She could have seduced the spies

into sexual acts, causing them to fall into sin. She could have set them up to be mugged. Rahab took a *major* risk. She risked her life and her family's life by lying to the wicked King and his men. The King of Jericho could have killed her on the spot and no one would have cared about this dead *prostitute*. You see, that is the beauty of it all. God did not see Rahab as a prostitute. He saw her as a misguided woman with great potential to usher in kings into the world. When you look in the mirror, what do you see? Regardless of what you think you see, God sees a beautiful created being, ready to express *greatness, positivity, and righteousness*. There you have it. God destroyed the city of Jericho, a fortified and powerful city, but Rahab and her *entire* family were spared from the cold steel of Joshua's sword. Not only was her family spared, but God allowed them to live within the congregation of Israel! What a blessing. When you make good decisions, your family is blessed in ways beyond compare. However, it does not stop there. Rahab had a child named Boaz. Boaz married Ruth. Boaz and Ruth had a son, named Obed and Obed fathered a son named Jesse. You might be thinking, *"What's the big deal, she had children. Based on her line of work I'm shocked that she didn't have a litter of offspring. I mean her business was sex and last time I checked, that is what was required to have children."* No, my friend, you are missing a *monumental* point! Let me finish the family tree she produced. Jesse fathered eight of his own children and named his baby boy David. Yes, that's right. King David. You know, the one who killed Goliath with a sling shot; the one who fell into sin with

Bathsheeba; the one who taught Solomon wise things; the author of most of the Psalms we read in the Scriptures; the one who God stated was a man after His own heart. Yeah, *that* David! Israel's greatest *earthly* King to date. Now let's keep it going. King David produced an earthly line as well, which includes none other than Jesus the Christ! You see, it does not matter how humble your beginnings or how complicated your family background may be, when a person makes the right decision to trust and follow the standards of God, the miraculous can happen. When God directs a person's life, a peasant (Rahab) can produce a King (David). That's equivalent to a Vulture (Buzzard) giving birth to a Bald Eagle (Majestic King of all Birds). God just asks that we make the right decisions to *change* our destination in life and in eternity. By the way, in Hebrews chapter 11, Rahab is mentioned again in the "Hall of Faithful Christians" who put their lives on the line for the Faith. No matter what you have been involved in or what you may be *currently* involved in, God is *able* to change your destination, if you *only* DECIDE to follow Him. My friend, remember; you have GREATNESS in you. You have to believe it. I don't care if you are smoking drugs, selling drugs, living a perverted lifestyle, or hate the things you have done in your past. God loves you so much he chose to be born in a *dirty, nasty,* and *common* stable competing with pigs, oxen, cows, horses, etc. He had to sleep amongst animals and manure. Imagine the stench, bugs, rodents and noise that his parents (Mary and Joseph) had to ignore and overlook in order to bring

Him into this world, feed Him, protect and comfort Him during his birth and early childhood. Do you see what I'm saying here? Jesus *humiliated* Himself in order to *buy* humanity back from the slave market of sin! God came in the form of a human to *identify* with the ills of humanity. No matter how *low* you've sunk in your life, God can go deeper than your lowliness. He can emancipate you from the *crack house*, release you from the *whore house*, and pardon you from the *jail house* and place you in the *church house*. Just put your trust in him. We are without excuse. Rehab *did not allow* her prostitution past to hold her *hostage*, but instead took control of her present and her future. Reflect upon these things.

Discussion Questions

1. Who was Rahab?

2. What did she do to "prove" her allegiance to God?

3. How was she rewarded by Joshua?

4. How did her decision to serve the God of Israel change her destination? (Hebrews 11)

5. What can you learn from Rahab's change of heart?

6. What does Rahab's story reveal about God's favor in a sinner's life who is willing to change?

7. Please list the reasons (excuses) why you can't become great.

Pillar 16: God is Never in a Recession

"However, we don't want to offend them, so go down to the lake and throw in a line. Open the mouth of the first fish you catch, and you will find a large silver coin. Take it and pay the tax for both of us."--Matthew 17:27 (NASB)

What is a recession? Well, according to Webster's Dictionary (2012) a **recession** is a *temporary* depression in economic activity or prosperity.[1] Right now, our country is swallowed in an economic recession, particularly for the working and middle class and I am feeling every pinch of it. The price of food has skyrocketed, gas is at four dollars a gallon, homes are being foreclosed, teachers are not getting raises, prescription medicine is increasing and the money is simply not coming in, as it should, to keep up with the rising costs of living. Something has to give. People are *still* losing their jobs. According to www.bloomberg.com, the U.S. unemployment rate is hovering around 7.6 percent. Crime sprees are taking this country by storm. Black on black crime is all over our TV screens. Military personnel are killing one another in training exercises. School shootings are canvassing this country's newspaper headlines. *Prisons* are built faster than churches and schools. More children in general are being raised by single mothers. Men are *marrying* men. Women are *marrying* women.

Times sure have changed. Mankind has re-defined the clear laws that God instituted. Post-modernism (No absolute Truth) has become the number one religion of America and criminality has become a new hobby. Nevertheless, the Christian's faith must remain steadfast in Jesus. It is through Him that all things hold together. Read **Colossians 1:15-18**:

> "15 *The Son is the image of the invisible God, the firstborn over all creation. 16 For in him all things were created: things in heaven and on earth, visible and invisible, whether thrones or powers or rulers or authorities; all things have been created through him and for him. 17 He is before all things, and in him all things hold together. 18 And he is the head of the body, the church; he is the beginning and the firstborn from among the dead, so that in everything he might have the supremacy. 19 For God was pleased to have all his fullness dwell in him, 20 and through him to reconcile to himself all things, whether things on earth or things in heaven, by making peace through his blood, shed on the cross.*" (NASB)

This is a powerful passage here. The Bible makes it clear Jesus Christ created the Earth and that He holds everything together. Check this out: Jesus Christ is the glue that holds all things in place. Some of you may say, "Yeah right." "How can Jesus really be holding things together when the murder rate in Chicago, Illinois is at an all-time high in 2012? People are still dying of AIDS across the world, young people are going to prison at an alarming rate, and street gangs are growing like cancer in poor and middle class neighborhoods. Furthermore, the God-ordained institution of marriage between a man and a woman is being *re-defined* by Congress, public schools, and *even* some misguided churches." "How can you say that Jesus Christ is holding things together?" Well, I think we look at the depravity of mankind and ask the wrong questions. As soon as it gets dark in life, our first inclination is to *blame* God or *erase* God from the equation of control and conscience. Well, let me ask you a few questions. Your body will sometimes suffer from sickness or illness before it goes to the grave. Have you ever had the flu? Have you ever suffered from strep throat? How about chicken pox? Have you ever broken a bone or sprained a knee? When you face an illness that takes you by storm, does your body "completely" shut down, or does it try to fight against the virus or bacteria that is in it? When you get to a point that you can no longer nurse yourself to heath, you go to the emergency room to get medicine that is prescribed by a licensed doctor. If that doesn't work, you admit yourself into a hospital, a place designed and created to care of the severely ill. You see, the Earth has a virus called SIN. The sin virus spreads upon *all* men (Romans 5:12). Now, like any other virus, sin has billions of strands and expresses itself in millions of ways in an individual. At this point, I want us to look a situation that was caused by sin, but used as an instrument of God to show that He is still in control, even though all Hell has broken loose! Please read the following passage taken from **2 Kings 4.**

The Drought and the Widow of Zerapheth (Elijah)

"1 Now Elijah the Tishbite, who was of [a]the settlers of Gilead, said to Ahab, "As the Lord, the God of Israel lives, before whom I stand, surely there shall be neither dew nor rain these years, except by my word." 2 The word of the Lord came to him, saying, 3 "Go away from here and turn eastward, and hide yourself by the brook Cherith, which is [b]east of the Jordan. 4 It shall be that you will drink of the brook, and I have commanded the ravens to provide for you there." 5 So he went and did according to the word of the Lord, for he went and lived by the brook Cherith, which is [c]east of the Jordan. 6 The ravens brought him bread and meat in the morning and bread and meat in the evening, and he would drink from the brook. 7 It happened after a while that the brook dried up, because there was no rain in the land. 8 Then the word of the Lord came to him, saying, 9 "Arise, go to Zarephath, which belongs to Sidon, and stay there; behold, I have commanded a widow there to provide for you." 10 So he arose and went to Zarephath, and when he came to the gate of the city, behold, a widow was there gathering sticks; and he called to her and said, "Please get me a little water in a [d]jar, that I may drink." 11 As she was going to get it, he called to her and said, "Please bring me a piece of bread in your hand." 12 But she said, "As the Lord your God lives, I have no [e]bread, only a handful of flour in the [f]bowl and a little oil in the jar; and behold, I am gathering [g]a few sticks that I may go in and prepare for me and my son, that we may eat it and die." 13 Then Elijah said to her, "Do not fear; go, do as you have said, but make me a little bread cake from [h]it first and bring it out to me, and afterward you may make one for yourself and for your son. 14 For thus says the Lord God of Israel, 'The [i]bowl of flour shall not be exhausted, nor shall the jar of oil [j]be

*empty, until the day that the Lord sends rain on the face of
the earth.'" 15 So she went and did according to the word
of Elijah, and she and he and her household ate for many
days. 16 The [k]bowl of flour was not exhausted nor did the
jar of oil [l]become empty, according to the word of the
Lord which He spoke through Elijah."* (NASB)

Now you may not be a Bible scholar, but the Prophet
Elijah was arguably the greatest Old Testament prophet who
ever lived! He lived in a turbulent time and conducted his
ministry throughout several famines. He was living near a
brook of water and God commanded the birds of the air to feed
him. Now that's great faith. To totally depend on God for your
every need is remarkable to say the least. As he journeyed along
the brook, his faith and dependence grew to unearthly levels.
However, a day came when his brook *dried up*. Now, it is easy to
say "Praise God", when in the back of your mind you know the
bills are getting paid, your health is stable, your children are
making good grades, your spouse is devoted to you and your job
is not threatened. But what do you do when the very things you
depend on are instantly snatched away *without* notice? How
would you respond if your vehicle was repossessed? How would
your faith hold up if your spouse told you that he or she wanted
a divorce? How would you behave if you constantly receive
phone calls and emails from your child's principal due to poor
academic achievement and behavior? What do you do when
your brook *runs dry*? Well, you actually have *two* fundamental
choices to make when you are faced with this type of crisis. You

can either *bless* God's name or *curse* God's name in your speech and your walk. Elijah did not curse God, but *humbled* himself even more and followed God's leading. My friend, in these dire and dry moments, God's voice is crystal clear in its calling. Are you listening for Him to speak to you? Now let's look at another prophet of God, *Elisha*, Elijah's successor.

The Widow's Oil (Elisha)

> "⁴ Now a certain woman of the wives of the sons of the prophets cried out to Elisha, "Your servant my husband is dead, and you know that your servant feared the LORD; and the creditor has come to take my two children to be his slaves." ² Elisha said to her, "What shall I do for you? Tell me, what do you have in the house?" And she said, "Your maidservant has nothing in the house except a jar of oil." ³ Then he said, "Go, borrow vessels at large for yourself from all your neighbors, even empty vessels; do not get a few. ⁴ And you shall go in and shut the door behind you and your sons, and pour out into all these vessels, and you shall set aside what is full." ⁵ So she went from him and shut the door behind her and her sons; they were bringing the vessels to her and she poured. ⁶ When the vessels were full, she said to her son, "Bring me another vessel." And he said to her, "There is not one vessel more." And the oil stopped. ⁷ Then she came and told the man of God. And he said, "Go, sell the oil and pay your debt, and you and your sons can live on the rest."
> (NASB)

Here, we have another account of a godly prophet, *Elisha*. He was the understudy and apprentice of *Elijah*. As discussed earlier, we *become* who we hang around. If you hang around a man or woman of God, it is pretty safe to say that you will take a similar path of godly living. If you hang around wise folk, you too will acquire great wisdom and understanding, which will assist you in making great choices. However, if you hang around lustful, blood thirsty, slanderous, scandalous, and greedy people the majority of your life: be warned—you too will take on the same characteristics and traits. This is one of the truest and purest principles of all time. I just love it because it is so fundamental in its assertion. Now let's look at this passage and dissect this. We have a widow who is forced into a situation she has no control over. That is, she has no *strong man* in her life to assist her in raising, leading, or teaching her sons the ropes of life. However, God, Who is able, sent her a man of God to step into her parental and financial drought. We also see a miracle of God through the widow's obedience to the command of God (get as many jars as possible). Think about this for one moment. God used what the widow *already* possessed to *prosper* her in her time of great need. God is the ultimate *Maximizer*. Do you know that one *dollar* ($1.00) in "God's" all mighty hand is superior to $100,000,000 in man's hand? I would like to introduce you to a powerful term called FAVOR! It is not the *resource* that opens the doors for the believer, it is the *God* of the resource that makes all things possible. When we understand this great distinction, we will take charge of our lives like never before. With God, miracles are the "*norm*," not the *exception*. Miracles to God are *equivalent* to brushing our teeth; it's an everyday thing. The widow was *stripped* of all hope, resources, and desire to live due to her *real* circumstances. God sometimes wants the same for us before he delivers in a mighty way. He specializes in pouring out miracles when *all* hope is lost. Do you feel hopeless right now? Do you feel that you have hit rock bottom? Do you feel that you only have one shot at having a *good* day, then you'll curl up and die?! Listen to me my friend, you are in the *right* position to get a miracle from the All Mighty God, but you must humble yourself and surrender to His way of doing things. This is where we all get into lots of trouble. We hit rock bottom and want to fuss and cuss about our dire situation. God *will not* move in an atmosphere of *foolishness* and *complaining* like that. We *must* do what the widow did, listen to what the situation is saying to your soul, and *follow godly directions* if you want to overcome it.

Now this is a key point I want you to see. The widow had to "do" her part for this miracle of God to work in her life. One, she had to seek out godly counsel (Elisha). Two, she had to follow his directives to the letter (find empty jars). Three, she had to believe in the *unthinkable*; that is, one jar of oil will fill a multitude of empty jars that are the same or of greater size. What are some of the things that you *already* possess? Is it a gift, a talent, a skill you possess which you have been *sitting* on, all this time? What I like about God is that He allows us to maintain our authenticity while working a miracle in our lives. We live in a world where people want to make others carbon copies of themselves or carbon copies of an ideology. However, God is not necessarily like that. Now, of course, He wants us to imitate Christ, but with the unique differences He created in us. The 11 disciples were true followers of the Messiah, but each one had his own way of doing things, their own personality, and their own style. When we meet people who want us to dress *exactly* like them, get a haircut *just like* them, talk like them, something is wrong with their theology. Remember, God has gifted each of us with something special that He wants to *maximize*, but it may take a *personal recession* for you to see what was *always* there, in order to emancipate you from your trap..

Discussion Questions

1. What is a recession? What does it mean to have a <u>personal</u> recession?

2. In both instances with the two widows, what did they have to do in order to achieve their miracle?

3. Does God want us to be carbon copies of one another or copies of Jesus Christ in our personal lives?

4. What hope do we have when we face an uncertain situation in our lives and we feel that all is lost?

5. How has this chapter assisted you in your personal life? How can you reach someone going through a personal recession?

PART V

BRACE YOURSELF: GET READY TO PROSPER

Pillar 17: Power of a Dream

"In my mind, I've always been an A-list Hollywood superstar. Y'all just didn't know yet."--Will Smith, Hollywood Super-star

Will Smith is one of the most exciting entertainers of our era. Movies, such as *Independence Day, the Men In Black Series, Hancock, ALI, and The Pursuit of Happiness* have pulled in over a billion dollars into the box office. It is estimated that he earns between $20-25 million dollars per movie plus royalties. According to Forbes Magazine, Mr. Smith's net worth is an estimated $250 million (www.forbes.com). Now that is big money! But this former 90's hip-hop rapper from Philly didn't start out as an A-list megastar overnight. It took a lot of *hard work, relentless effort, belief in his skills,* and *doors of opportunity to open.* Equally important, one thing remained constant for Mr. Smith. Whether as a rapper or sitcom actor, he treated all of his roles as if they were his last. He didn't allow his skin color to become a barrier to becoming a multi-million dollar super star. He didn't let Hollywood *politics* pigeonhole him into exploitive roles that many African American actors found themselves trapped in (i.e. drug pushers, pimps, athletes, servants, or criminals). He set his eyes on becoming the *leading* man. And he accomplished this very feat with distinction. Now this Pillar is *not* to focus on *Will Smith*, but to express the principle of *"believing in yourself."*

You see, there is a *link* between *how* you view yourself and how the world will *end up* viewing you. If you view yourself as a loser, then those in your environment will do the same. It's one psychological mirror. Think about this for a minute. When you look into a mirror it is silent. You are the one who decides whether you look fine or not. Our environment is like a mirror. They will only treat us the way we *"feel"* about ourselves. Nothing more, nothing less. It's quite simple when you really think about it.

In Walt Disney's 1976 popular elementary story of The *Little Engine That Could,* we see the powerful truth of believing in *personal* abilities. That is, believing in one's God-given abilities and skills. It is quite amazing how wisdom can be right under our noses if we make an effort to search for it. The book tells the story of a *red* train engine that carried a host of children's dolls and animals, including a very special funny *clown* doll, to good children who lived on the *other side* of a large mountain. During her journey, she suddenly breaks down and can go no further. The *funny clown* toy decided to jump out and look for a *solution.* He stood on the tracks with a red flag in his hand to flag down help. The first train that approached him was a shiny gold luxury coach train. This train was full of luxurious amenities and plenty of room to accommodate the stranded toys. The clown pleaded with the luxury train for assistance. The gold shiny train told the clown that he wasn't going to help the "likes" of you and left. The other dolls were saddened and distraught, but the clown did not give up hope. He noticed a strong black freight train coming towards the broken down train. The clown pleaded with this train too. The freight train stated that he was strong and carried heavy cars and machinery over the mountain, but was not going to the carry the likes of the toys across. He steamed off into the sunset, refusing to help the red train. Third, the clown spotted another train chugging down the tracks, this time an old, *black,* rusty train. The clown, with the same mindset to secure help, asked the old train for assistance. The old train, remarked, *"I cannot, I cannot. I am too tired and need to rest my weary wheels."* He slowly rolled away refusing to help the broken down red train, saying to himself, *"I cannot, I cannot."* Finally, the clown noticed a little *blue* train chugging down the road. With the same motivation and cheerful attitude, he flagged the little blue train down and pleaded with her. The little blue train stated that she was not the biggest, for she just switched trains in the yard. However, she offered to help the red train and the children's toys over the mountain. As she hitched up and began to chug up the mountain, she stated to herself, "I think I can, I think I can." As she consistently told herself what she could do, the faster her wheels rotated. With encouragement from her passengers, she reached the pinnacle of the mountain and began her descent. However, her vocabulary changed. Instead of saying "I think I can", she stated

"I thought I could, I thought I could." Consequently, the toys made it to the good children on time!

Now why did I take to time to summarize this popular story? Well, I'm glad you asked. Let's break this down to the nuances. There are several key characters in this critical story: *a red train, a gold shiny train, a strong black train, an old, rusty train, the blue little engine and the funny clown doll.* I want to use my imagination as I interpret this story as it relates to *my* life. To me, the red train symbolizes those people in our lives like our parents, our upbringing, and significant individuals who plant seeds of greatness in our lives as young children and teenagers. These are the fundamental principles of life that are handed down to us as we grow up in society. Principles, such as *"Treat everyone right."; "Always show forgiveness."; "Make good grades in school."; "Get as much education as you can before you become old, etc."* However, there comes a time in all of our lives when we must "leave the nest" and live our lives on our own, hopefully, applying the principles taught to us by our elders and sage instructors. The red train also represents, to me, a door way or a bridge towards personal success. Notice, the train was already headed in the mountain's direction, but it did not intend to go over it, just stop at the foot of it instead. Let me tell you something, my friend, we will have people in our lives for only a *season* of time. They were not designed to stay with us forever, but they were assigned to us by God to lead us to the foot of the mountain of success. It is up to us to have the *happy clown* mentality. That is, we are to "find" a way to get *over* the mountain. The gold luxury train, to me, represents the social circles or echelon of persons who may not want us to achieve success and prosperity. They are surrounded and inundated by resources, fortune, opportunity, power, and privilege. Yet, because you and I *may not* be from the *same* side of the "tracks" (*no pun intended here*), they look down upon us with disdain, contempt, mistrust, or even bitter hatred. The *strong black* train represents those who have the ability to assist us, but refuse to do so because they are consumed with what they have *worked* hard to garner for themselves. The black train was not gold and shiny, but it *still* found a way to build power to help itself "easily" scale the mountains of life. This is the type of person that swears by the mantra, *"I pulled myself up by my own bootstraps."* Although this person was not "given" success, it is critical to note that it is not right for them to become "stingy" with their success. Then there is the old, black, rusty train. This train represents a "self-pity" mentality. Of all the trains in the story, this train simply stated, *"I cannot, I cannot, I cannot...I am too tired ...My wheels are too weary."* As long as you live, many of the people you encounter will be like the old, black engine. They do not "live" life, they simply exist within "life." They go day after day, week after week, month after month, year after year focusing on what is *not* going right in their lives, the challenges they face in life, and the *absence* of key people in their childhood that set them up for failure. Now, I'm *not* saying that negative events are not *real*, but c'mon man, it's time to realize that if you have Jesus in your life as Lord and Savior, you can do *all* things via His power.

You are never at a disadvantage as long as you commit to "*grinding*" at your dreams! Grinding means to roll up your sleeves and fight for your dreams with everything you got. You must develop this type of belief system. That is, you must chase personal success (*while keeping God first*) over everything! Until you get this type of tenacity, you will never achieve what God has set you to achieve, but it will take (a) *work,*(b) *effort*, (c) *sleepless nights*, (d) *fasting*, (e) *praying*, and (f) *just plan blood, sweat,* and *tears*! But you must look in the mirror and *know* your vision and mission for your life, my friend. Finally, the most important character of them all is the funny clown. That's right, you thought I was going to say what *everyone* says, the little *blue* engine. Nope. In fact, the little blue engine was a *result or consequence* of the funny clown's *relentless* and *resilient* efforts to "make" a way out of nothing. Now let me tell you how significant the clown was. One, he was the only doll/toy to jump out of the red train once it broke down. All of the other animal toys stayed in the "safety" of the train cars, just "wishing and hoping" for the best, but not the clown. He knew a secret that all "successful" people know. That is, he knew that success has to be *hunted* down like a trapper entices big game. You see, he didn't care about *how* others viewed or perceived him, (*only* a colorful funny clown). It didn't matter what the gold train, strong black freight train, or even the old train thought of him. Instead, he focused on achieving the impossible. He didn't take no for an answer. His resilience was so strong, his passion so overwhelming, and his grind so thorough that success had *no choice* but to come his way. As long as you live, you will have *some* critics tell you that you are just a C.L.O.W.N. (**C**owardly, **L**ow- quality, **O**rdinary, **W**eak, **N**on-existent); a nobody; a second-rate whatever, but don't let this low expectation *stop* you. Like the clown in the story, rejection should make you *hunger* even more. That's right; just like Michael Jordan stated, "*My pain was my motivation.*" You see, pain is a *major* part of life that none of us can escape. Realize that you cannot escape hurt, disappointment, and mistreatment. This is not your fight. Your fight is with *success, not* with *pain.* Pain is like the red train that forced the clown to jump out and have the courage to put it all on the line to get the results he desired. So next time you look in the mirror, my friend, ask yourself if you are the colored train or the funny clown. Know who you are. Write down your dreams. Don't take no for an answer! God bless you.

Discussion Questions

1. What does the *blue* train represent?

2. What did the *strong black* train represent?

3. What did the *gold, shiny* train represent?

4. What did the *funny clown* doll represent?

5. What did the mountain represent?

6. Read **Ecclesiastes 9:10**. What is this scripture saying to you right now?

Pillar 18: Damascus Experience

"Crises don't make appointments to visit us, nor do they reschedule"--Dr. Lamont Ricks

Damascus. What in the World is Damascus? Well, in the Book of **Acts chapter 9**, a devout Jewish official named Saul of Tarsus had orders to hunt down individuals who professed their faith in Jesus Christ (The Way). On his mission along the way, he had an interesting encounter with God! Please read the following passage and check back in with me:

> *"9 Then Saul, still breathing threats and murder against the disciples of the Lord, went to the high priest 2 and asked letters from him to the synagogues of Damascus, so that if he found any who were of the Way, whether men or women, he might bring them bound to Jerusalem.3 As he journeyed he came near Damascus, and suddenly a light shone around him from heaven. 4 Then he fell to the ground, and heard a voice saying to him, "Saul, Saul, why are you persecuting Me?"5 And he said, "Who are You, Lord? "Then the Lord said, "I am Jesus, whom you are persecuting. It is hard for you to kick against the goads."6 So he, trembling and astonished, said, "Lord, what do You want me to do? "Then the Lord said to him, "Arise and go into the city, and you will be told what you must do."7 And the men who journeyed with him stood speechless, hearing a voice but seeing no one. 8 Then Saul arose from the ground, and when his eyes were opened he saw no one. But they led him by the hand and brought him into Damascus. 9 And he was three days without sight, and neither ate nor drank." (NASB)*

Ananias Baptizes Saul of Tarsus

"10 Now there was a certain disciple at Damascus named Ananias; and to him the Lord said in a vision, "Ananias. "And he said, "Here I am, Lord."11 So the Lord said to him, "Arise and go to the street called Straight, and inquire at the house of Judas for one called Saul of Tarsus, for behold, he is praying. 12 And in a vision he has seen a man named Ananias coming in and putting his hand on him, so that he might receive his sight."13 Then Ananias answered, "Lord, I have heard from many about this man, how much harm he has done to Your saints in Jerusalem. 14 And here he has authority from the chief priests to bind all who call on Your name."15 But the Lord said to him, "Go, for he is a chosen vessel of Mine to bear My name before Gentiles, kings, and the children of Israel. 16 For I will show him how many things he must suffer for My name's sake."17 And Ananias went his way and entered the house; and laying his hands on him he said, "Brother Saul, the Lord Jesus who appeared to you on the road as you came, has sent me that you may receive your sight and be filled with the Holy Spirit." 18 Immediately there fell from his eyes something like scales, and he received his sight at once; and he arose and was baptized.19 So when he had received food, he was strengthened. Then Saul spent some days with the disciples at Damascus." (NASB)

Saul is a Changed Man

"20 Immediately he preached the Christ[c] in the synagogues, that He is the Son of God.21 Then all who heard were amazed, and said, "Is this not he who destroyed those who called on this name in Jerusalem, and has come here for that purpose, so that he might bring them bound to the chief priests?"22 But Saul increased all the more in strength, and confounded the Jews who dwelt in Damascus, proving that this Jesus is the Christ." (NASB)

The Jews Try to Kill Saul

> "23 Now after many days were past, the Jews plotted to kill him. 24 But their plot became known to Saul. And they watched the gates day and night, to kill him. 25 Then the disciples took him by night and let him down through the wall in a large basket." (NASB)

Saul of Tarsus at Jerusalem

> "26 And when Saul had come to Jerusalem, he tried to join the disciples; but they were all afraid of him, and did not believe that he was a disciple. 27 But Barnabas took him and brought him to the apostles. And he declared to them how he had seen the Lord on the road, and that He had spoken to him, and how he had preached boldly at Damascus in the name of Jesus. 28 So he was with them at Jerusalem, coming in and going out. 29 And he spoke boldly in the name of the Lord Jesus and disputed against the Hellenists, but they attempted to kill him. 30 When the brethren found out, they brought him down to Caesarea and sent him out to Tarsus." (NASB)

The Church Benefits From Saul's Life Change

> "31 Then the churches throughout all Judea, Galilee, and Samaria had peace and were edified. And walking in the fear of the Lord and in the comfort of the Holy Spirit, they were multiplied." (NASB)

Here we see a serious minded, intelligent, and ruthless individual take pride in hunting down disciples of Jesus Christ and murdering them. However, on this particular journey, he ran into a gigantic problem. This was not just any problem, but a problem that he could not solve. He had a run-in with God All

Mighty! That is, when he met God, he was "knocked" off his high horse. What is your high horse? Is it money? Is it racism? Is it sexism? Is it elitism? Is it greed? Is it pride? Is it success? Is it privilege? Is it hatred? Is it gossip? Is it status? For Saul, it was *Religion*. He was a devout Pharisee, meaning he studied the Laws of Moses to the letter. He was a teacher of the Law, but he did not have a *Relationship* with God, which only comes via Jesus the Christ. God introduced Himself to Saul, blinded him, and gave him a "new" mission and direction for his life. As a result, God changed Saul's name to Paul the Apostle. Many of us were just like Saul of Tarsus. We were dead in our sins, confused, haters of God and His standards, or focused on our own terms of life, but God had to "knock" us off our high horse, blind us to our road of disaster, and re-set us to do His will. I can tell you many stories of people who were totally against the will of God: murderers, rapists, racist bigots, cheaters, thieves, prostitutes, blasphemers, etc. Years ago, I heard a powerful story of a former Ku Klux Klan member who converted to Christianity in the South. Not only did he renounce his past, he also did something that certainly blew my mind. He voluntarily placed himself under the leadership of an African American Pastor of a mixed-ethnicity church in the South. There are stories of ex-drug pushers, ex-prostitutes, and ex-drug addicts who *encountered* Jesus Christ on their personal Damascus Road and totally changed their lives for the cause of the Gospel. Now, I don't want to lead you in the wrong direction here. You do not have to be a *criminal* or come from the *bottom* to qualify for a Damascus Road experience. I know of Christian missionaries, street preachers, and ministers who earned advanced college degrees, were making six-figure incomes, owned several real estate properties, to have a Damascus Road experience. You see, regardless of what walk of life we derive from; rich or poor, moral or immoral, educated or uneducated, we all have had a personal Damascus road experience. The blessing in all of this is that no matter how wicked or sinful someone may be, God has a way of "knocking" them off their high horses of life, causing them to exchange their identity from an *enemy* of God to a *servant* of God.

Now what is a Damascus Road experience? Well, it is *any event* that *drastically* changes the course of one's life from a man-planned orientation to a God-planned orientation. It also includes utter helplessness and immobility. Notice, when Saul was knocked off his high horse, he heard a voice and was blinded for three days. He asked a life-changing question: *"Lord, what would you have me to do?"* This is the overall *goal* of a Damascus Road Experience. You will face this pertinent decision; to do God's will *or* continue to do your own "thing." He had to be led to the place God instructed him to go. Another truth about a Damascus road experience is that you still have a choice to follow the way of God, or continue to disrespect the All Mighty One.

Another important point to note is God *always* sends one of His saints into the lives of those who have had a Damascus Road experience. We see in the text that God spoke to Ananias in a vision. In his vision, God instructed him to meet Saul and pray over him, but Ananias, knowing Saul's reputation, questioned God out of fear. I can't say I blame brother Ananias for asking God some questions. I appreciate this because Ananias was being *real* with God. It's not always easy to do what God commands because we don't always know the full extent of His purpose. However, we are still called to obey the voice and leading of God in our lives. Ananias thought God was sending him on a suicide mission by asking him to meet Saul, for Saul was a ruthless man who killed Christians for sport. This is like asking a black preacher to meet a white supremacist and pray over him. Now that's scary! But you cannot underestimate the power of the LORD. Let me give you an example. Every day we hear miraculous stories where men and women gamble all of their money away, or escape the hot bullet from the gun of an enemy, or overdose on a drug only to be resuscitated by the doctors, or escape a tragic car accident, etc. Nevertheless, as soon as things ease up, they continue to live in a way contrary to God's standards. However, those who respond correctly to a Damascus road experience are changed from the inside out. This is an act of the Holy Spirit's power. He changed everything people, but individuals must "humble" themselves under the mighty hand of God for a Damascus road experience to change their lives. When you look back over your life, that is, some of the mistakes and choices you've made, or the close calls with death you had, can you say that you've encountered a Damascus Road experience? Maybe you didn't realize that a particular event which almost took you out was really God calling you to "walk" in His ways. Maybe you thought it was luck, fate, or chance. No my friend, that was a Damascus Road experience.

Discussion Questions

1. What is a Damascus Road experience?

2. How did Saul respond to God's call on his life?

3. What part did Ananias play in the conversion of Saul?

4. Why did Ananias question God about seeking out Saul?

5. What did God say to Ananias regarding Saul's conversion?

6. What should be one's proper response to a Damascus Road Experience? (vv. 6-7)

7.   What was the outcome of Saul's Damascus Road
     experience? (vv. 20-22)

Pillar 19: Victim's vs. Victor's Mentality

" I can do all things through Christ who strengthens me." –
Philippians 4:13 (NASB)

This pillar is one that is dear to my heart. Have you ever heard of people always blaming the "Man" or blaming their parents, or their ex-spouse for all of their current woes. Well, in this particular chapter, we will analyze two contrary *belief systems* that can have an indelible mark on all of our lives. The two belief systems are (1) a victim's mindset and (2) a victor's mindset. What is a mindset? Well according to Webster's Dictionary (2012), a **mind-set** is a *fixed* state of mind.[1] Now, the word *fixed* means to be cemented. Normally when a contractor builds a fence or a deck, he will often use concrete to cement the wooden or metal posts into the ground. Why does he do that? It's quite simple. Any good contractor worth his/her weight in salt will test the ground where s/he desires to build. He will consider several factors or variables, such as slope of the yard, acidity of the soil, hardness of the soil when wet, minerals/ composition of the soil, and even the pests that live in the yard. Once it has been determined that the soil is suitable to build upon, the contractor must decide how deep to dig the holes and how much concrete or cement to use to affix the poles. The stronger the concrete, the stronger the gate or deck. My friend, a *mind-set* is the mental "cement" on which *all* decisions are made and followed.

A Victim with a Victor's Mentality

In most cases, a victim can control his/her mentality. Notice, I said most cases here. Children of abusive parents would qualify as a case in which a small child does not have the control necessary to change their environment. This is an exception to the rule. What I am referring to are teenagers, young adults and even older adults who go through life complaining and blaming other people, their circumstances, or the government as to why they have not achieved their God-created potential. This is my target audience here. I want us to look at the real-life story of a woman who did not allow her real circumstances to shut her down. Although very real, her illness *did not* stop her for doing all she could to reach Jesus, her source of assistance. Please read Luke 8:43-48 and check back in with me.

> *43 Now a woman, having a flow of blood for twelve years, who had spent all her livelihood on physicians and could not be healed by any, 44 came from behind and touched the border of His garment. And immediately her flow of blood stopped.45 And Jesus said, "Who touched Me? "When all denied it, Peter and those with him said, "Master, the multitudes throng and press You, and You say, 'Who touched Me?' 46 But Jesus said, "Somebody touched Me, for I perceived power going out from Me." 47 Now when the woman saw that she was not hidden, she came trembling; and falling down before Him, she declared to Him in the presence of all the people the reason she had touched Him*

and how she was healed immediately.[48] And He said to her, "Daughter, be of good cheer; your faith has made you well. Go in peace."

I chose this story for several important reasons. For one, we have a woman here during Biblical times, meaning she was not treated equally to men. It is important to note that in many countries today (2013) women are still not treated equally with their male counterparts. She was considered a second-rate citizen, as this story took place in a Middle Eastern town. Second, she spent all of her earthly resources and money on finding a cure for her constant blood flow (menstruation). Third, as a woman with this particular condition, she was considered ceremonially unclean by Jewish standards and customs. Fourth, she found herself in an overly crowded area full of people who were bigger, stronger, and physically healthier. Have you ever been to a large event, like a concert, sports contest, or motivational speaking conference, where hundreds or maybe thousands of people are trying to meet the singer, athlete, or speaker? It can be quite a task for the most skilled and persistent individual. Your energy can quickly wane and your patience and hope can wear thin fast. However, an element is implied in this text that many people overlook. You see, it is not enough to be persistent in seeking a solution to your problems, what one must have is a "do or die" mindset when attacking their fears and chasing their dreams. Ask yourself the following questions: *"Do I feel that I will cry many tears if I do not chase my dreams with every thread in my body?", and "Am I willing to put it all on the line to break this negative cycle in my life?"* Questions like these are gut wrenching but are supremely necessary before you can ever reach your personal potential in this life. I want you to catch what I'm about to say here. Are you ready for this? Are you sure? Well, okay. Check this out: *"You must break through in order to get a break through."* Don't steal my quote, now. Think about what I just said to you for a moment. Look over the precipice of your past and think about all of the things you could've accomplished or achieved. Think about all of the places you could've seen. Think about all of the interesting people you could've met, particularly ones who would have added *wisdom, significance,* and *fulfillment* in your life. Imagine the job opportunities that would have *your* name all over them had you given your *all.* Imagine the business venture you could've secured had you *not* given up on yourself. Nevertheless, you SETTLED for being a VICTIM of your circumstances, your past mistakes and failures, *others'* low expectations of you, and your past limitations. The 'breakthrough' statement is so *simplistic,* yet so *profound.* When you fully understand and apply this simple truth, you will be able to achieve the *impossible* in your personal life and in your relationships. Can I be transparent with you, my friend? Okay. I *need* to lose about 35 pounds, but my *desire* is to lose about 50 pounds. I know what it takes to lose this amount of weight (e.g. drink more water, cut out red meat, snacks, and greasy foods, and exercise daily). God has even blessed me to have the necessary fitness equipment in my garage necessary to achieve this goal. But if you know like I know, a garage gets very cold in the winter and extremely hot and humid in the summer, and let's not forget those spiders and bugs during the summer months. Now, every day on my way to work, I see certain men and women running for miles in the rain, ice, heat, and even the snow. While I'm in the comfort of my vehicle with the heat blasting or the A/C blowing, I see the same people overcoming the elements. As a result of their diligence, consistency, and perseverance, they are in *better health* and *earned* the right to sport very attractive physiques. What is it that *drives* these people to get up *early* in the morning, put on layers of clothing, open the front door and run in freezing winter weather or in the blazing sun? It's quite simple. These successful individuals have considered themselves *dead* to the *negative* or *harsh* realities that surround them. That's right, these runners are *fully aware* of their uncontrollable circumstances. They are fully cognizant that the cold icy wind is blowing in their faces, yet their *discipline* to run *outweighs* the cold, uncomfortable temperatures outside. There "discomfort" outweighs their "comfort." When you are more concerned about "comfort" you will end up in 'discomfort.' Like the woman with the issue of blood who *knew* that she was a *second-class citizen* and *insignificant* to many did not allow that to stop her from her blessing, that is, her healing from God All Mighty! Sometimes you have to fight your way *through* the circumstances to get

God's attention. You have to fight through barriers that were *designed* to keep you down, keep you silent, keep you inferior, keep you confused, and keep you ignorant (un-informed) to the truth. She considered herself *dead* to the crowd, *dead* to the naysayers, *dead* to the criticism, *dead* to the sexism of her day, and *dead* to her own illness (bleeding). While all of the aforementioned items were real, serious, and costly, she overcame them *all* to reach God's heart. You can do the same! It's all in how you *view* life and what lens you *choose* to look through. Success *can* be achieved, promotion can be had, quality relationships can be had, education can be had, and physical fitness can be had. You have to go after it and do *whatever* it takes to get it with *every* drop of sweat, blood, and tears. You *can* break through the barriers with God on your side.

The Mule and the Farmer

I am often reminded of the story (parable) of an old mule and the farmer. I have added *emphasis* to this story. The story speaks of an old mule that went to get water from a well, but somehow fell into it. The farmer heard the loud panic-filled cries of the mule. The farmer tried to wrap a rope around the mule and pull him up, but the mule was too heavy, and he was wedged tightly inside of the well. After several efforts to rescue the desperate mule, the farmer gave up. The farmer reasoned to himself, "This mule is old and dumb. All he's good for is carrying trash and baskets on his back. I can't sell him, for he is too old. I cannot eat him because no one desires *mule meat.* I guess I have no other option but to kill him." The farmer thought of ways he could kill the mule, but then he came up with a brilliant idea. "I know what I'll do! I'll just bury him alive in the well! That will be sure to shut him up; plus I can get another one for cheap!" The farmer decided to take his shovel and began to throw dirt into the well. The mule noticed that the farmer, who he placed his trust, was trying to bury him, so the mule decided to do something extraordinary. As the dirt landed on the mule's back, he would simply shake off the dirt and pat it under his feet. The more dirt the farmer threw on the mule, the more he shook off the dirt and pat it under his feet. After a few hours, the mule began to elevate towards the top of the well. The farmer just kept throwing dirt and the mule just kept shaking off the dirt. Finally, the mule reached the top of the well and jumped out of it to safety. To the farmer's surprise, the mule escaped certain death by using the dirt the farmer threw on him as the *means* of deliverance. That is, he used the dirt and the mud to his *advantage.* In this life, you will encounter many haters, that is, people who will throw all kinds of harsh dirt your way in an effort to bury you alive through depression, slander, and under low expectations, fear, your past failures, racism or elitism, or the pressure of perfection. However, I'm here to tell you that these are *all* lies. It is all a massive smoke screen and an illusion, unless you *choose* to believe it. Think about that for a second.

The farmer did not consider the mule as *relevant* or *significant* to his plans, making his life expendable, but the old mule *"broke through"* the barrier of *insignificance* and "made" himself *relevant* to the farmer. We must take this *valuable* lesson from the mule. If a rusty old mule with *low* intelligence can *turn* the tables on the wise farmer, think of how much *more* "you" can achieve in your life. *Now* is the time for you to take *personal inventory* and write down all of the things that make you *unique, strong, beautiful, intelligent, savvy, wise*, and *significant*. You may feel that you were born in a **dark well**. Maybe your parents abused or deserted you; maybe you failed to graduate from high school; maybe you got involved in drugs; maybe you got involved in prostitution; maybe you caused great pain in the lives of your children; maybe you betrayed your spouse's trust; maybe you turned your back on God. It's never too late to rewrite your life's story, or at least change the last chapters. It's time to *encourage* yourself and get out of the well! You must develop a mentality of a *victor*, not a victim. Your life and future hope *depends* on it.

Discussion Questions
1. What is a victim's mentality?

2. What is a victor's mentality?

3. What must a person do to secure a personal breakthrough' in their lives?

4.   What causes people to form a victim's mentality?

5.   What can we learn from the *mule* in the story?

6.   What steps did the mule take to ensure its survival in a dark well?

7.   What were the farmer's intentions?

8.   What were the mule's intentions?

9.   Did their intentions match?

10. If a person is in a dark well of life, is curling up and dying his or her "only" option? Why or why not?

11. What was the woman with the issue of blood willing to do to get to Jesus? (pp. 146-147)

Pillar 20: God Doesn't Wear a Watch

"The hardest thing to do is turn your cares over to God, completely."--Dr. Lamont Ricks

God *does not* wear a watch. Wow, just think about this statement for a minute, look over the course of your personal life, and remember all of the times God stepped in and delivered you from destruction. Think about the times God spared your life from certain pain and death. Give some thought to the blessings He brought to you that you had abandoned. You see, we cannot view God All Mighty in the same way we view humanity. Please read the following passage taken from **2 Peter 3:7-9**:

> *⁸ But, beloved, do not forget this one thing, that with the Lord one day is as a thousand years, and a thousand years as one day. ⁹ The Lord is not slack concerning His promise, as some count slackness, but is longsuffering toward us, not willing that any should perish but that all should come to repentance."* (NASB)

Did you read that? Let's look at verse eight. A thousand (1000) years to the Lord God is the same as one day? What does that mean? Now before we go into this, we need to fully understand who we are talking about here. Many times, we *give up* on praying to God, our dreams, or achieving the impossible because

154

of one important variable, TIME. Time waits for no one. In a nutshell, time is the *most* passive-aggressive phenomenon known to man. That is, it seems to move too slow and too fast at the same time. For example, as I write this book, I am 36 years of age, married with children.

Time has surely gone by. My kids are growing like trees and I'm starting to see more gray hair in my head and in my mustache. Where did all the time go? However, I still remember *my first-grade* birthday party at *Camelot Elementary* School like it was only yesterday. During that time, I wanted to be a teenager so bad, but now, my teenage years are far behind me. Do you see what I mean here? When I was a young boy, I wanted to become a young man, but now I am headed towards middle-age adulthood. Time, slow down, please! Everything we do in our lives is solely based upon *time*. One thing I always tell the people I talk to is that *"crises do not make appointments to visit us; they just show up."* Now what is a crisis? *A crisis is any event that causes us great pain, distress, worry, or confusion within a given period of TIME.* A crisis brings great stress because time is at stake. Let me give you a few examples here. Say you go to the doctor and he or she says that they have found a tumor and it is cancerous. What is the first thing that will hit you mind? Exactly. *How long* do I have to live before this cancer eats my body away? Right? Everything in your life will *instantly* change based upon this *new* information. Will you *forgive* the people in your past, or take that expensive vacation? You might *hug* and *kiss* your children every day and tell them you love them dearly. You might stop worrying so much about all of your bills, school loans, and car notes. You might *stop* drinking liquor, smoking drugs, or using profanity. You might start attending church every Sunday and join the choir. You might become a frequent volunteer at the local Nursing Home. The things that used to tick you off will no longer have *psychological influence* in your mind. Now how could such a drastic lifestyle change happen so instantly? I will tell you how; impending death. You see, in our heart of hearts (our souls), we know what we need to do to have a better relationship with the Creator. Sometimes we need a crisis in our lives to get our attention as to why we are really here-- *to serve God and make the world a better place.*

Now, suppose, you visited the doctor and he or she said that they found a cancerous tumor, but you have about 70 years before it starts to metastasize. Although no one wants to hear the mighty "C" word, I am sure you would not have the same level of stress associated with this news because there is *so much time* associated with it. Time *controls* everything we do in this world. It controls how we live, move, think, play, *and* decide. So being that time controls crises, why do you and I need to know that *God does not wear a watch*? Simple, He is God. He *created* TIME for humanity. Since He created TIME, He is not subject to TIME or its laws of limitation. And since He is not subject to it, He is *not* stressed out by it either. The following is a brief list of the effects of the laws of TIME:

- *Decay*
- *Weakness*
- *Frustration*
- *Death*
- *Old age*
- *Out of style*
- *Loss of Relevance*

- *Antiquated Knowledge*
- *Rust*
- *Hopelessness*
- *Grief*
- *Anger*
- *Irritation*

Have you ever felt the consequences of TIME? In case you didn't understand, what generation are you from? Are you a baby boomer? Are you a generation X-er? Are you a generation Y-er? Just by virtue of your answer tells me that you are under the law of TIME. But with God, He never gets old; He never sees decay in any form. He will never die. He will never go out of style. His knowledge is complete for *all* time zones and eras. He is *never* in a crisis. He never loses His power and might. His frustration level is "0" because He is Self-Existing and Self-Satisfying. That is, He is the Sovereign Ruler of TIME itself. Before we can really appreciate who God is, we must be sure we know some of His characteristics and attributes. Do you know that when you understand the attributes of a person, your treatment of them changes according to their understood attributes?

For example, if I told you that there were loose dogs roaming your neighborhood, what would you do? Well, first, you would remain in your home until you verified that you saw the dogs. Second, you would ask me *"what types of dogs are loose?"* If I told you it was a *Toy Poodle and a Chihuahua,* then you would not have a problem leaving your home, getting into your car, and handling your daily business. However, if I called you to tell you that the two dogs consisted of a *Pit Bull* and an adult *Rottweiler* I am sure the entire situation would change. You would probably lock your door and stay put until the community *animal control officer* comes out. If you absolutely *had* to go outside to check the mail or get an important item out of your car, you would probably grab a baseball bat or a large stick-just in case one of the dogs decided to attack you. You would be completely immobilized within the four walls of your home. Why the change of heart? I'll tell you why, *attributes*. That is, the attributes of the small dogs are vastly different from that of large more aggressive dogs, such as Pit Bulls and Rottweilers. Both of the large dogs are able to severely injure children and adults; they are able to lock their jaws and take down a 300 lbs. man with little effort. That's why you would change your view point. Your mother did not raise a fool.

When it comes to God, we need to know His attributes by reading His Word, The Bible. He is able to create out of nothing; He is able to manipulate nature and natural laws to accomplish His purpose. He is able to change the physical properties of matter whenever He chooses. The sea obeys Him; the Sun and Moon obey Him; the Animal kingdom obeys Him; the rocks obey Him; even TIME obeys Him. When you know how powerful He is (Omnipotent), you will *adjust* how you approach

Him. You don't want to raise your fist and shake it at Him; you wouldn't want to curse His name and you will be careful how you complain about His workings in your life. Take for example the story of the prophet Jonah. Because of his disobedience, God called a large fish from the deep to swallow Jonah whole without killing him. The fish took him under water for three (3) days until Jonah got the message that he was dealing with Almighty God. Once Jonah repented of his disobedience and rebellion, the fish vomited him upon dry land (see **Jonah chapter 1:4-17; 2:1-10**). Now, the last time I checked, humans can not breathe underwater without oxygen. In addition, fish cannot live on dry land. We seem to have a paradox or oxymoron situation. Since a fish *cannot* live on dry land (breathe air like we do) and a human being *cannot* breathe under water, then how did a fish take a man underwater for "three" consecutive days and he live off of little to no oxygen? Furthermore, how could Jonah have the strength to pray verses 2-9 with limited oxygen and zero light? God stepped in and manipulated the laws of nature, which includes TIME.

There are some things that you pray to achieve, but you feel that TIME is *running* out on you. It might be a new business venture, a newborn baby, a job promotion, finding the love of your life, or for your wayward son or daughter to find their way. Whatever it is, just realize that God dwells *outside* the realm of TIME and He does not need a watch to go by in order to bless you in your life. Simply put your trust in Him completely and watch Him do the impossible! God is able.

Discussion Questions

1. Why is it important to know that God is not controlled by TIME?

2. What is the definition of a crisis?

3. How should we view God when TIME is running out in our lives?

4. Read **Genesis 18**. What did the ANGEL of the LORD promise Abraham and Sarah in their old age? (vv. 1-15)

5. How did Sarah respond? (vv. 10-12). Was she being *realistic* in her thoughts about this promise?

Pillar 21: Position Yourself for a Blessing

"We can learn a lot from a Praying Mantis: get in position, pray, then jump at the opportunity."—Dr. Lamont Ricks

Well, I see you finally made it to the end— the last chapter of this book. I hope you were able to pick up some valuable nuggets of wisdom. I decided that it is best to finish off strong by talking about *Positioning*. I don't know anyone who does not *want* or *need* a blessing in their personal lives. I am sure you can stand to be blessed in your life, am I correct? Position means *everything* when you are trying to accomplish your goals in life. We hear of all kinds of stories about proper positioning. One that comes to mind is *Cinderella*.

In summary, Cinderella was raised in an *unfavorable condition* that was designed to keep her subjugated (oppressed) and limited. The persons who should have been the ones who would guide her towards success were the very ones who caused so much *grief* in her life. Day after day, month after month, year after year, Cinderella was *constantly flooded* with low expectations, verbal abuse, and was locked away in her room. She was *not* to be seen or heard when company came over because the powers that kept her oppressed were *jealous* of her looks and potential. Jealousy is one of the most evil conditions humanity can express. Like a raging fire, it grows to *uncontrollable* levels, torching its victims with no mercy. The evil step-mother and step-sisters knew full-well that had Cinderella been *properly exposed and trained to* engage the prince, she would have crushed the competition, so they poisoned her mind by constantly telling her that she was "worthless." Has anyone in your past, maybe a *parent, boyfriend or girlfriend, teacher or guidance counselor* ever called you "worthless?" Maybe these individuals made you *"feel"* worthless by their actions towards and low expectations ascribed to you. The tongue loaded with poisonous speech can carve deep emotional scars in our psyches.

What a way to live. Many of us know the story. A ball (dance) is announced for the Prince to select his bride. Hundreds of would-be princesses prepared their best garb, but Cinderella, having *no* support or sponsor, cried out for *assistance.* Although she did not have any human help, she had a fairy godmother who heard her cry. The fairy godmother stepped in and "maximized" what Cinderella had for that one 'perfect' night. That is, the fairy godmother gave her an OPPORTUNITY. If you know Jesus as your Lord and Savior, you don't need a fairy godmother; you have the REAL DEAL. He is God All Mighty. Do you need God to open up a door of OPPORTUNITY for you? Do you need God to step in and block the fire of *guilt, pain, and past failures* from burning down your success? Do you need God to create a bridge over turbulent waters of uncertainty in your life? Do you need God to provide you with a *sound mind* so you can get a good night's rest? (2 Timothy 1:7) Well if you need God like I do, then cry out to Him consistently and fervently (Luke 18:1-8). If you are His child, He will answer your cry in *His timing*, but remember *He does not wear a watch.*

Cinderella had to take full advantage of the MOMENT, for by time the clock struck 12 AM, she would return to her current disenfranchised position in society. What did Cinderella do? She POSITIONED herself for the Prince to notice her and the rest is history. Her entire life and destiny changed all because she positioned herself for a blessing. You see, when an opportunity comes "knocking," you don't have TIME to *cry* about what you don't have, or to *complain* about your upbringing. You don't have time to *cuss and fuss* about not having a father growing up, or to *gripe* about how society mistreats you. You don't have time to *discuss* your past failures or bad decisions you made. OPPORTUNITY is a *non-emotional* phenomenon. It does not have a brain or feelings. It does not emote. It has abstract qualities associated with it and is very fluid. It simply comes and goes, like a rare bird that perches on a tree limb. If you blink twice, it has flown away. It *does not care* about your *fears, upbringing, failures, mistreatment, laziness, low self-esteem, depression,* or *unbelief*; it is only concerned about POSITION to seize a blessing.

When it comes to POSITIONING we must think of the three *P's: (1) Prayer, (2) Patience,* and *(3)Preparation. Prayer* is critical to attaining access to the Heavenly Father, Who is seated in High places. Prayer is how we communicate with God. It is our language of hope and supplication to the Master. *Patience* is a key ingredient needed to secure our blessings in this life. Patience is not an easy road to take. In fact, patience is the *most difficult* of the three P's, by far. God is not moved by our squirming, complaining, and fussing about the length of time it takes to deliver a blessing in our lives. This is where so many of us get into a heap of trouble. We pray, cry, and pray some more. We consult with our friends, family, and the religious leaders in our churches, only to find that God is *not* moving an inch—so we think. However, God is *always* moving. Do you know that the Earth in *constant* rotation? This rotation is a critical factor in gravitational balance, weather, and high tidal flooding. This rotation is so subtle that we cannot feel Earth moving with our feet, or see it moving with the naked eye, but God allows the sun to set and rise at specified times of the 24 hour day. Whether we see it or not, the Earth is always moving for our protection against G-forces that would cause bodily harm. Similarly, God is *always* moving, my friend. We may not see it yet, but he is moving in ways unbeknownst to us. In His time, He will expose the blessings we have been eagerly praying for, as long as it is His will. Finally, *preparation* is the lynch pin to securing blessings from God. In the book of Genesis chapter 2 you will notice that God gave Adam a job (naming the animals and tending and cultivating the garden) before He brought him EVE, his wonderful blessing. Preparation is so important that one cannot and should not expect to receive his/her full blessing until they have adequately counted the cost, changed the way they think, and laid a firm foundation for the specified blessing.

The New York and Boston marathons are two of the most popular and prestigious races in the world. They are approximately 26.2 miles long. I get tired just thinking of jogging 1 mile! It takes a very disciplined group of athletes who are in elite physical condition, just to train for this monster of a race. It takes months, even years, to train effectively for a race of this magnitude. Every year over 40,000 participants from all over the world pay thousands of dollars just to enter into this contest. They are super bowls of Marathons.

Suppose a man thinking within himself, *"I can do this. I'll just go to the local high school track and run four laps (1 mile) a day for 26 days, then I'll be ready for the marathon. I'll just drink a lot of Gatorade and water while I train and I will be able to compete."* Do you think this man will be ready? I'll answer this for you. NO! Why? Because in order to *adequately* train for a marathon, you must run several miniature marathons until you can run the distance of the race you wish to enter. That is, you must work your way up to running 26.2 miles.

Many of us are praying to God 2 to 3 times a week, expecting Him to just jump up and answer us like a genie in a bottle. God is not a wish-wizard; He is the Creator of all things. Some *men* are praying for a wife to love and live out the rest of their years with, but men, are you preparing for her like Adam prepared for Eve? Are you making sure your *health, house,* and *heart* are in order to *protect, provide, prosper,* and *praise* her for the rest of your days? If not, then *don't* expect God to bring her to you anytime soon. You must be persuaded in your own mind that God is able and that He can bless you. Once you have prayed earnestly, you must walk as it is already done! Bottom line, you must run your own "spiritual" marathon so you can identify and receive your blessing. It will be painful. It will seem never ending at times. It will sting your spirit. It will burn at your conscious, but keep trusting in God and working while you wait on the Lord to renew your strength and bring you your blessing!

The Praying mantis is one of the most enigmatic creatures in the world. It is a predatory bug that helps with the ecosystem in many ways. The larger species of Praying mantis eat the likes of frogs, snakes, rodents, bugs, and small birds. It will eat whatever it can grasp. What makes the praying mantis *unique* is its ability to camouflage itself to fit into the natural environment. It will make itself look like an innocent leaf or plant pedal in the wind. Do you know that in Australia, some species of praying mantis can turn black in color after a fire has consumed the dry land? They do this to adapt to the environment of fire charred wood pieces. Once an unsuspecting prey comes near, it will pounce on it, killing it with its pincers. You see, when it comes to positioning, you have to have the Praying Mantis mindset. You have to do what it takes to succeed.

You have to make the necessary adjustments, no matter how harsh your environment. You have to develop patience. You have to ignore all of the distractions that hold you down and keep you from focusing on what matters most. You have to position yourself in *any* condition until the OPPORTUNITY comes your way!

Conclusion

Well we have come to the end of *21 Pillars of Power*. It has been a great journey. We have looked at real, relevant, and relational passages of scripture. We learned that there is nothing new under the sun. Life goes in one big circle. Every culture and era of time faced the same problems we face today, just with minor differences. It is my earnest desire that you gained more knowledge, understanding, and excellence of mind. You know, the mind is an idea-generating factory that we all possess. Empowerment comes from within, but opportunities to be empowered come from God. Some of you have decided to make changes in your life due to the power of the Scriptures used in this book. I hope you stay focused on the Lord. Some of you have decided to cut off the dead-end relationships in your life. Although difficult, you've made up your mind to achieve greatness, all without parasitic people in your circle. Some of you reaffirmed the course you are currently navigating. You now know that you are worth it. Why? Because Jesus Christ gave His life for you to live the abundant life. Remember, God has given you *power to love, power to live, and power to prosper!* Until we meet again, POWER UP!

ABOUT THE AUTHOR

Dr. Lamont Ricks is a motivational speaker, minister, educator, and author. He has an extensive background in School counseling and Educational leadership. He currently works as an Assistant Principal in a Virginia Public School Division. He is also an adjunct professor at Regent University's Graduate School of Education in Virginia Beach, Virginia and Associate minister at his local worship center. He has spoken to middle and high school students on the subjects of *college readiness, career planning, bullying, self-esteem building, goal setting, conflict resolution,* and *decision-making strategies.* Dr. Ricks has an unwavering passion to see young and older readers alike find ways to reach their highest level of success and self-worth. It is through his writings, speaking, and ministering that he endeavors to empower, encourage, engage, edify, educate, and expose his audience to achieve the impossible. POWER UP!

NOTES

CHAPTER 2 (PILLAR 2)

1. Dr. Eldon Taylor, *Choices and Illusions: How Did I Get Where I Am, and How Do I Get Where I Want to Be?* New York, New York: Hay House, Inc., 2007)

CHAPTER 6 (PILLAR 6)

1. MERRIAM-WEBSTER ONLINE (www.Merriam-Webster.com) copyright © 2013 by Merriam-Webster, Incorporated. Term: *Parasite*

2. MERRIAM-WEBSTER ONLINE (www.Merriam-Webster.com) copyright © 2013 by Merriam-Webster, Incorporated. Term: *Parachute*

CHAPTER 8 (PILLAR 8)

1. MERRIAM-WEBSTER ONLINE (www.Merriam-Webster.com) copyright © 2013 by Merriam-Webster, Incorporated. Term: *Collateral*

CHAPTER 16 (PILLAR 16)

2. MERRIAM-WEBSTER ONLINE (www.Merriam-Webster.com) copyright © 2013 by Merriam-Webster, Incorporated. Term: *Recession*

CHAPTER 17 (PILLAR 17)

1. Watty Piper, *The Little Engine that Could.* New York: Platt & Munk Publishers, 1976).

CHAPTER 19 (PILLAR 19)

1. MERRIAM-WEBSTER ONLINE (www.Merriam-Webster.com) copyright © 2013 by Merriam-Webster, Incorporated. Term: *Mindset*

CONTACT & BOOKING INFORMATION
To book Dr. Ricks for your next speaking event, please send an email request to:

1. info@drricksempowers.com or
2. drricksempowers@gmail.com

Please type in "**Booking Request**" in the subject line.

TWITTER: Follow Dr. Ricks on Twitter for motivational quotes: **@DrRicks2**

Visit our Website at: www.drricksempowers.com
Check out our blogs at: www.drricksempowers.com/blogs

ORDERING INFORMATION:
Visit: www.Amazon.com to order your copy of *21 Pillars of Power.*

Here are just a few examples of how *21 Pillars of Power* can be used to encourage, inspire, and impact your students, business staff, family members, athletic team, church members, and/or those you love:

- Devotional Resource
- Christian growth Resource
- Educational & Counseling Resource
- Graduation Gift
- Marital Resource/Wedding Gift/Couples Resource
- Personal Success Resource
- Sunday School Text (ages 15 and up)
- Men's ministry Resource
- Women's ministry Resource
- Motivational Resource
- Self-help Resource

- College student Inspirational Resource
- A stocking stuffer, birthday gift, or anniversary gift
- And much more....

MY THOUGHTS & REFLECTIONS

Directions: This section is designed "just" for you. Please use the space on the following pages to write down any of *your* dreams, thoughts, ideas, and goals. If you have a vision, you must *write it down* and *run with it.* This is your time to reflect on the *21 Pillars* and use them as launching pads towards spiritual and personal success. POWER UP!